America Challenged

America Challenged

The New Politics of Race, Education, and Culture

Rosalie Pedalino Porter

ROWMAN & LITTLEFIELD
Lanham • Boulder • New York • London

Published by Rowman & Littlefield
An imprint of The Rowman & Littlefield Publishing Group, Inc.
4501 Forbes Boulevard, Suite 200, Lanham, Maryland 20706
www.rowman.com

86-90 Paul Street, London EC2A 4NE

British Library Cataloguing in Publication Information Available

Library of Congress Cataloging-in-Publication Data Available

ISBN 9781475865325 (cloth) | ISBN 9781475865332 (pbk.)
| ISBN 9781475865349 (ebook)

To my younger generation who will make this world measurably better: David Pierce Gamliel, Carley George Porter, Addison Rose Gamliel, Emily Avery Porter, Finn Cooney Porter

"In the final analysis, our basic common link is that we all inhabit this small planet. We all breathe the same air. We all cherish our children's future. And we are all mortal."

—President John Fitzgerald Kennedy, 1962

"Don't trust in your own righteousness; practice moderation in food and drink; and don't worry about things done in the distant past."

—St. Anthony, North African desert monk, 4th century

Contents

Foreword

The struggle against the Left on racial matters—in which I include politically correct race-based decision making, identity politics, and the related and supporting ideologies—is part legal and part cultural. Dr. Porter covers it all in this powerful book.

The stakes are high indeed. When you think about it, what, besides protection from foreign enemies, is more important to our country's long-term health than making sure Americans are not divided into racial or ethnic enclaves, but instead share fundamental common values and see each other and themselves as, first and foremost, Americans? America always has been a multiethnic and multiracial nation and is becoming even more so; this makes it imperative that our national policies not divide our people according to skin color and national origin. These policies should emphasize and nurture the principles that unify us: *E pluribus unum*—out of many, one.

In this foreword, I offer briefly some additional and related thoughts that overlap with and complement Dr. Porter's more thorough and developed ones.

***

The legal part of the struggle with the Left here is straightforward enough and is going tolerably well. Conservatives—and, indeed, the overwhelming majority of Americans—oppose the use of racial preferences, which are now legally constrained to a degree but still far too common in education, employment, and contracting; and we oppose the use of the "disparate impact" approach in the enforcement of our civil-rights laws, which is likewise constrained but not nearly enough. I'm reasonably optimistic right now that we will continue to make progress—maybe even dramatic progress, particularly with the issue of racial preferences in higher education now before the Supreme Court.

But my optimism is cautious and depends very much on who is appointing our federal bureaucrats and, especially, our federal judges. The legal struggle still very much hangs in the balance. Elections have legal consequences.

The cultural part of the struggle is more complicated, and its outcome even more uncertain. On the one hand, the general public overwhelmingly rejects the notion of racial essentialism and its supporting, often Marxist-derived ideologies. Yet the academy and mainstream media are on the other side, and there is little willingness among corporate leaders to take politically incorrect positions. Most politicians, too, are timid here. They should be bolder in challenging the cancel culture. They should read Dr. Porter's book.

***

Before we can choose a path, we must know where we want to go. Before we can set public policies, we must know what kind of public order we want. Defining our goal is a particularly instructive exercise with respect to race relations. The overwhelming majority of Americans want the United States to be an unbiased nation. That is, we would like individual Americans not to be bigoted, and we would like our government—federal, state, and local—to be unbiased as well. To achieve that goal, it is not necessary for Americans to be literally colorblind. People will still notice skin color, just as they notice hair color or eye color. But it wouldn't influence behavior and treatment. People will still be proud of their ethnicity, but blackness should be no more important than perhaps Irishness is today. The cultural differences will be minor and intermarriage rates will be high.

And Americans would subscribe and want other Americans to subscribe to certain basic principles. Years ago, I made a list of my "top ten" of them; as I recall, this was prompted by considerations of immigrant assimilation, but they apply to all of us, native and immigrant alike:

1. Don't disparage anyone else's race or ethnicity.
2. Respect women.
3. Learn to speak English.
4. Be polite.
5. Don't break the law.
6. Don't have children out of wedlock.
7. Don't demand anything because of your race or ethnicity.
8. Don't view working and studying hard as "acting white."
9. Don't hold historical grudges.
10. Be proud of being an American.

The job of conservative think tanks and intellectuals is to provide and distribute intelligent support for all this, and pushbacks against the Left. That's what Dr. Porter has done with her book (and, I might add, it is also the mission of the Center for Equal Opportunity, which is the organization that introduced me to Dr. Porter).

***

Let me spell out a bit more the pernicious sorts of political correctness that conservatives like Dr. Porter and me are talking about. It's the notions of "white privilege" and "institutional racism" and "mass incarceration"; the mindset of diversity *uber alles*; the 1619 Project approach to American history; and the notion that those who reject the Left's positions on "sexual orientation" and "gender identity" are hopeless bigots.

Thus, for example, we are told that being opposed to racial preferences is now racist. Think about that. And saying you think the best qualified individual should be admitted to school, hired for a job, or awarded a contract—that's racist, too. Amazing. Now, as I say, I think most of this is happily rejected by the general public. That's the good news, even if our elites are loath to say so. But, on the other hand, it's scary the inroads being made in the K–12 system regarding U.S. history and sexual orientation/gender identity.

Let me also note briefly here that none of the Left's agenda would be even remotely attractive to anyone except for the presence and persistence of racial disparities—and really only those disparities involving African Americans. But the way to address these disparities is not by pretending that the reason for their persistence is "white privilege" or "institutional racism" or anything like that. Rather it is by recognizing the real reason for the persistence of these disparities, which is cultural—particularly the catastrophic out-of-wedlock birthrate among African Americans (seven out of ten, and even higher in many urban areas).

Indeed, pretending that the main problem is privilege rather than culture (having children outside of marriage is fine, crime is cool or at least not the criminal's fault, etc.) makes it less likely that the culture problem will be seriously addressed. And an important aside here: cultural problems of this sort are moral and, therefore, a province that calls foremost for actions by churches rather than governments.

***

There's a powerful subtext in the Left's approach to American history: "You should feel bad about yourself and your country because people of your color did bad things once upon a time to people of another color." The idea is to intimidate and to shut people up, the better to advance the Left's agenda. But this backward-looking message is not good for race relations, being all about blame, envy, and resentment, about feeding guilt and refusing to forgive.

Nor is a backward-looking focus a helpful one for African Americans in particular. The following analogy might be apt. Suppose that an *ante bellum* Southerner criticized Yankees for having bad manners. He might well have been right. But, in hindsight, we would all agree that, bad manners or not, the Yankees were right about slavery, and to focus on bad manners at a time when that abhorrent institution was alive and well showed, to put it charitably, a lack of perspective.

Or, to give a funnier example, recall the scene in the movie version of Mel Brooks's *The Producers*, where the Nazi playwright is bemoaning the fact that Churchill is more fondly remembered than Hitler, notwithstanding the fact that Hitler was a better dresser, a better dancer, and a better joke-teller. Well, maybe, but still . . .

In 2022, for the Left to be focused on renaming buildings and removing statues—when seven out of ten African Americans are being born out of wedlock, and *that* is the real obstacle to black progress—shows a similar lack of perspective. To live well and prosper, the focus must be on seizing opportunities in the present and preparing for the future, not obsessing over wrongs in the past.

***

So the key to designing a pathway forward on race relations is, duh, to focus on the future and not the past. That's true in what the laws should say and how they should be applied, and it's true for broader cultural and policy—and simply personal—considerations as well.

Personal analogies can be misleading in public policy, but there is one useful one here: It's not a good idea to focus on the misfortunes of your past and what might have been. It's better to focus on what you need to do going forward. It's just not that complicated. Can any sane person really believe that race relations will be improved by, say, starting a system of reparations and further institutionalizing PC racial preferences? No: What's needed is to fight racism of both the PC and old-fashioned kind.

Again, it's not that complicated: Treat people as individuals. Don't generalize about them because of their skin color or what country their ancestors came from. It may be true that, when you meet an African American young male, he is statistically more likely to have recently committed a crime than an Asian American older woman you meet. It may be more likely that the non-Hispanic white is more likely, again as a statistical matter, to have led a life of ease and privilege than a Hispanic you meet. But there are so many exceptions, and it is so unfair, that it's wrong to generalize. Again, treat people as individuals.

It's not that complicated. There's a time for subtlety and nuance and balancing tests and considering the totality of circumstances—but there's also a time for bright lines and simplicity and clarity. And race relations are in the latter category:

- Treat people as individuals—don't treat people differently because of their color

For this to happen, good men and women have to speak out. Dr. Porter has done that, and in doing so has taught others how to do so as well.

Roger Clegg

Roger Clegg (JD, Yale Law School, 1981; BA, Rice University, 1977) is a lawyer who now serves with Dr. Porter on the board of directors of the Center for Equal Opportunity, where he was formerly president and general counsel. Mr. Clegg now has a Christian blogsite, MerePensees.com.

Preface

At this moment in our country's social history, when so much is changing so rapidly on so many fronts, it is imperative to address the forces and trends that have led us to our nation's troubling cultural conditions. For a younger audience, it is instructive to review the years of radical social activity from the 1960s onward and chronicle the positive achievements. For a more mature readership, there is a more balanced assessment of America as a complicated nation, much less racist than it is judged to be by its radical critics.

The past two decades have documented a reversal in the aspirations for social changes affecting minority populations. The coronavirus period and the George Floyd incident have grossly accelerated national upheavals on cultural issues. There is an urgent need for analysis and commentary, and for presenting viewpoints not much favored in the mainstream press.

In my first book, *Forked Tongue: The Politics of Bilingual Education*, I highlighted an education policy that was a documented failure and the politics of immigration and ethnicity that kept it in place. My work played a significant part in changing laws in three states: California, Arizona, and Massachusetts. My continued advocacy for immigrant children, in state and federal courts, and before the U.S. Congress, has led to positive improvements.

Being there matters. Having the good fortune to live through one of the most volatile periods in U.S. history, the past half century, confers some benefits. Reviewing historical events personally experienced, at a distance of time and place, allows larger patterns to emerge to enrich current perceptions.

We are not at *The End of History and the Last Man*, as Francis Fukuyama glibly asserted in his 1992 book, far from it. Fukuyama argued that the end of the Cold War and the fall of the Berlin Wall in 1989 somehow marked the endpoint of evolving human history. No more ideological battles with Communism—Western liberal democracy established forever. He spoke far too soon, as we know from the international battles over religion since 2001 and the clashes over culture and identity in America since.

We are in a perilous period. We are in a struggle for the American soul. It would be folly to concede the high ground completely to the "systemic racism" mob at the cost of diminishing our democratic principles.

My goal in writing this book is to provide factual data from different viewpoints. The aim is to present an open, varied, civil public dialogue from a side that is not given much attention, due to the power of cancel culture and other ideologies that control our public discourse. From my early professional life, I have sought out the causes of social problems, especially in public education, and offered possible solutions. These searches warrant the sharing of my knowledge with others, as in the current writing.

This book is intended for an educated adult audience, from both sides of the political divide. The ideas and evidence provided are expected to be of interest not for academics only but for a wide general readership. There is some sense that growing numbers of people find the monopoly in the mainstream press of the "woke" progressive hegemony to be unsatisfying. There is not enough variety of thought out there for an informed debate on cultural issues of great importance to our country's continued progress.

America Challenged: The New Politics of Race, Education, and Culture could be a useful supplementary reading in academic departments in the social and political sciences, ethnic studies, gender studies; diversity, multiculturalism, feminism, anti-racism, equity, and inclusion courses. It provides a needed contrast to the current raft of publications promoting one uniform idea of an irredeemably racist nation to be transformed or overthrown.

Most of my adult life has been centered in an academic community, with some periods of living in other countries for professional work. But my life experiences are far broader than just college town USA. Coming to this country as an immigrant child, learning the language and ways of a new culture, prevailing over poverty and difficulties of family adjustment, and achieving moderate success in my chosen profession—these testify to the opportunities implicit in my personal "American dream" experience.

Popular progressive "wisdom" to the contrary, we are still overwhelmingly the "land of opportunity." The ability to climb the ladders of betterment and success are very much within the reach today of all with the will and the drive to pursue them.

Acknowledgments

First, I am indebted to my three sons, Tom, Dave, and Steve, for their unstinting love, attention to my work, and support for this book project. They all inherited their late father David Porter's love of writing. They read various segments of my project with professional care. My largest share of gratitude is due to Tom, the eldest. He offered me a shelter during the early months of coronavirus lockdown and contributed his editorial and tech skills throughout the entire composition of this manuscript.

The era of the pandemic certainly had an influence on the creative process, in contrasting ways. Almost all professional, social, and extended family in-person activities were restricted, and this allowed daily work hours to expand—a mixed blessing.

Academic friends who read drafts of this book and offered advice and support include Roger Clegg, Center for Equal Opportunity; Johanna Haver, consultant to the Arizona Department of Education; Paul Mariani, Poet, Emeritus Professor of English, Boston College; Ricardo Munro, California educator; and Christine Rossell, Professor Emerita of Political Science, Boston University.

The ProEnglish organization in Washington, DC, offered me extended support, allowing me release from my board responsibilities for several months, thanks to special help from Dale Herder and K. C. McAlpin. Stephen Guschov and Stephanie White of the ProEnglish staff provided research assistance.

I am grateful to friends and colleagues who read and gave valuable comments on one or more chapters and enthusiastically urged me onward: Nadine Gallo, Laura MacLeod, Eileen Mariani, Helen Anne Nyberg, Jerry Nyberg, Lisa Pedalino, Charles Pfiel, Louise Pfiel, Blanche Browne, and Laura Medenbach.

Appreciation for Tom Koerner at Rowman & Littlefield for seeing the potential of this project, and to Kira Hall for editorial assistance in turning it into a viable product. University of Massachusetts graduate student Nefteli Forni Zervou was a crucial assistant in the early formatting and editing process.

1

Introducing the Issues

"A great civilization is not conquered from without until it has destroyed itself within. The essential causes of Rome's decline lay in her people, her morals, her class struggle, her falling trade, her bureaucratic despotism, her stifling taxes, her consuming wars. The political causes of decay were rooted in one fact—that increasing despotism destroyed the citizen's civic sense, and dried up statesmanship at its source."

—Will Durant, *The Story of Civilization* (Vol. III)

American society has undergone substantial cultural changes since the 1960s, a decade of social upheaval unrivaled, perhaps, until 2020. The half century since has produced economic growth, broader educational opportunities, and legal movements to firmly realize the long overdue civil rights of African Americans, to finally redress the evils of slavery and the Jim Crow years.

These large social improvements in U.S. society, however, were accompanied by negative developments, as traditional community structures have been steadily eroded—family cohesion, religious participation, standards of public and personal behavior.

Americans are by nature infatuated and passionate about the new—ideas, fashions, movements, creeds, and technological inventions. Often these headlong passions lead us to grossly overdo the well-intentioned novelties. The collection of essays that follows will focus on several broad areas.

Redefining our common history and culture has gained momentum over the decades, starting in the academy and spreading throughout our public expressions. This is the kind of atmosphere prefigured in the worst times of the Stalinist purges. Tearing down or defacing the statues of national figures, especially but not limited to those monuments of Civil War leaders, has become a popular sport of college students.

A national movement to denigrate the contributions of most Whites, reserves a special disapproval of straight, White males. The value of science and of neutral, evidence-based knowledge is now in question. Even science must hew to an agreed-on ideology, only considered reliable if it is given racial and gender-sensitive perspectives.

Our world has experienced the overturning of the values of family, religion, and community, not only in the United States but in all Western societies, with all forms of Christianity especially under attack. Beginning fifty years ago, efforts to raise people out of poverty were enlarged. Government projects such President Lyndon Johnson's "Great Society" invested heavily in what promised positive results.

The actual outcomes of these good intentions had unintended consequences. By later measures and reports, they created a permanent underclass, with government support for destructive personal behavior. With the advent of affirmative action, new rights were created giving special privileges to certain minority groups in college admissions, jobs, and contracts.

The beginning of official racial categories to recognize who deserved special rights was meant to be temporary, for a defined period only, but in the past few decades it has become almost impossible to terminate. It is accepted practice to apply different standards for judging behavior and to determine the punishing of disruptive or dangerous behavior according to the race of the perpetrator. Out of this climate of competing rights has emerged the establishment of the concept of White privilege, to be opposed by any means, the popular new racism.

Attacks on our inalienable right to speak and write our minds, the crowning glory in our Bill of Rights, for some peculiar reason is severely under attack from the "woke" progressives on the left. Was it not the righteous activists on the far left who originated the "free speech" movement in the 1960s, *pace* Mario Savio at U.C. Berkeley? The descendants of the former fighters for free speech are now in the vanguard of those calling for the denial of free speech for any ideas they do not approve. This is a puzzling and unwelcome development in a free society.

Yet attacks on speech are now generated and predominant in academia, the place to explore and vigorously debate various perspectives. Now it is the closing of the academic mind. The social media conglomerates rule daily life and enforce their biases without fear of challenge, never more obviously than in both the run up and the follow up to the 2020 election.

The feminist/women's liberation movement initiated in the late 1960s won instant recognition and a high level of participation in our college town. Its original aim was to promote equality of the sexes in education and careers. Very soon it evolved from that call for equality to enforcing women's dominance. It became routine to denigrate men and to enshrine women, especially the most privileged, with every advantage.

In the last few decades, the feminist agenda has expanded to creating new, gender-bending definitions of thirty-five or so different sexual personae. The biological sex of human beings that has been recognized for a million years, or whatever number we put on the emerging of our first ancestors, is no longer acceptable. In our schools, children are instructed from their earliest years to recognize and respect whatever sexual persona may be presented and to be "sensitive" to all at all times.

An elementary school principal was instructed, in a private interview with parents, that their eight-year-old boy in a third-grade classroom must be referred to as "she" on Mondays, Wednesdays, and Fridays, and as "he" on Tuesdays and Thursdays, by his teacher and classmates. The parents were indulging their child in the trendy new ways of gender identification.

In the universities and colleges, gender and ethnic "victim studies" programs proliferate, beefing up the "intersectionality" craze, to analyze oneself to determine how many ways one is a victim—the more, the better. The feminist movement has essentially come full circle in three quick steps: (1) from a movement to bring women to equal status with men, (2) to the power grabs by feminists, (3) to the renewed view of women as victims, weak creatures needing special care and protection.

Race, that terrible scar on American society, the national sin of slavery, the shame of the Jim Crowe years and segregation, all received new consideration beginning in the years after World War II. After desegregating the armed services, the next aim was to address desegregating our country completely, making equality for Blacks a fact supported by laws and judicial rulings.

The first repairing of our guilt over discrimination was the desegregating of our schools (*Brown vs. Board of Education,* 1954), workplaces, housing, and transportation. It was strongly resisted, openly defied, in various parts of the country, with well-reported bigotry of public officials in Alabama, Arkansas, and Boston, to name a few prominent arenas of resistance. But the federal government fought these illegal efforts and finally prevailed.

The NAACP and many respected Black civil rights leaders of those years risked harsh treatment in public, and the history of those years is both deplorable and finally triumphant. The efforts of one of the greatest Americans of the twentieth century, Dr. Martin Luther King, Jr., to promote a color-blind, integrated society, resulted in his assassination. It is a national tragedy that many in Black leadership of the past two decades have been intent on power, guilt-mongering, exploiting, and increasing racial divisions. They are turning back the clock on all the improvements and bringing us to more negative race relations.

Fully analyzing the coalition of circumstances that contribute to upending our Western values is a very tall order. Elements of some of the defined issues overlap. It is difficult to tease out, for example, the part played by identity politics in race relations, attacks on free speech, campus life—in fact, in just about every one of the major areas at issue.

Is the culprit to be blamed for all this, the decade that holds prime place for the most upheavals in modern times, the 1960s? The furies that characterized that decade have gathered momentum in the present day. The actual elephant in the room is not merely the sixties decade but Marxism.

A case can be made that the steady growth of this ideology (though it calls itself democratic socialism or social justice or other deceptive titles) has gained currency, thanks to the influences of a coterie of forceful "woke" leftists. Not least, especially in the most recent decade, is Black Lives Matter whose founding principles are anti-capitalist, anti-nuclear family, anti-religion, and whose leaders have publicly declared themselves to be a pro-Marxist organization.

One of the most dangerous and corrosive forces affecting every area of our nation today may very well be identity politics and its hulking, bully enforcer—critical race theory.

The essays presented here address the major social issues summarized above, with an attempt to understand the world recently created and some thoughts on effecting a modest change of course, going forward.

Damaging Effects of Multiculturalism, Multilingualism, and Diversity Policies on American Public Life

The United States, since its earliest years, has been a multiethnic, multilingual country with a societal ideal that generations of newcomers accepted, each group of new arrivals adapting, fitting in, and thriving, perhaps in one to two generations. This unifying ideal was challenged in the 1960s when the very notion of "assimilation" became anathema, deemed an attack on personal identity. This essay proposes that three closely related concepts—multiculturalism, multilingualism, and diversity—influence legislation, court rulings, and education policy, which in turn serve as agencies of formation and conformity to the new orthodoxy. In 2022, the new mantra is DEI—diversity, equity, and inclusion—and are the only measures deemed reliable for judging the acceptability of every area of American culture.

DIVIDING US OFFICIALLY BY RACE AND ETHNICITY

The rejection of the "melting pot" metaphor bred the new imperative to remain as separate, identifiable groups—a "salad bowl." This notion was not introduced in the 1964 Civil Rights Act and the 1965 Voting Rights Act. The notion of dividing us as a nation, by law—*temporarily*—into five groups, was the work of federal bureaucracies (for example, the U.S. Census data) and judges, and has progressed over decades:

- African Americans—an oppressed minority, the original group for whom civil rights legislation was intended, to redress the evils of slavery

- Native Americans—also an oppressed minority, various tribes, various languages
- Hispanics—a newly invented title, creating a power bloc of new arrivals from thirty-five different countries who share a language (official subgroups: Hispanic-White, Hispanic Non-White), most of whom have not suffered discrimination in this country
- Asians/Pacific Islanders—a bloc representing people from a variety of countries, cultures, and languages
- Whites—the prevailing majority, including but not limited to the dominant elites, of Western European origin

The first four groups were identified for official protected status, with preferences in hiring and in admission to higher education. The naming and renaming of groups is further discussed in the essay that follows on identity politics.

The basis for this "affirmative action" was to correct for a history of discrimination against African Americans and Native Americans. Legitimizing "positive discrimination," might be temporarily justified, but why extend such privileged status to people who had just arrived in the United States from, say, Korea or Argentina or Panama?

No distinction is made, for example, between upper-middle class arrivals from the Dominican Republic or Costa Rica and the poor, uneducated arrivals from El Salvador or Haiti—all are equally entitled to preferential advantages. A more detailed description of the evolution of group identities in our nation is provided in the identity politics essay.

EDUCATIONAL SEPARATISM: LANGUAGE EDUCATION MANDATES

The ethnocentric, multiculturalist agenda has played a damaging part in the field of education since the end of the 1960s. A section of the Elementary and Secondary Act of 1968, the Bilingual Education Act, was intended "not to maintain separate languages but to help Mexican kids learn English." Instead, it spawned a radically new, substantially separate education for children who lack a full command of the English language, an estimated 5 million students in U. S. public schools today.[1]

Massachusetts passed the first Transitional Bilingual Education Act in 1971, forcing schools to teach non-English speakers in their native language for years, delaying their learning of English. Sixteen other states soon followed suit. Massachusetts then added "bicultural" to the state regulations, specifying that the history and culture of each student's country of origin must be incorporated into classroom lessons.

At a time when the integration of African American students was vigorously pursued, a separate program was organized for non-English-speaking children, taking time away from academic content learning for "feel good" language and culture maintenance. Two-thirds of English language learners are Spanish speakers, but the rest are from 322 different language backgrounds.[2]

In a typical urban school district, the non-English-speaking children often represent a dozen different native languages and countries of origin, even though the largest percentage are Spanish speakers. No attempt to teach the so-called "history and culture" of each group can reasonably be incorporated into the typical school day. The idea of promoting the culture of various native lands during the school day was unworkable as it meant reducing the teaching of other school subjects.

There were certainly teachers and school administrators who understood the folly of this "bicultural" intrusion into their classrooms, but they were mainly silent as the programs had loud political support. The United States already provides the shortest school day and school year of any developed nation. Taking time away from reading, math, or science throughout the school year would not benefit children.

A fundamental dislocation occurs when people move across borders. There must be an understanding among even the least educated that adaptations and adjustments to new ways will have to be made. The notion in the bilingual/bicultural education programs of the 1980s and 1990s to pretend that families can maintain their original languages and cultures in a completely new environment was a delusion.

Educators hewing to the progressive ideas imagined a multilingual, multicultural stasis, everyone staying put, not mixing and melding in the ways of earlier generations of new entrants to the United States. New York University professor of philosophy Kwame Anthony Appiah is well known for this oft-quoted statement from his *New York Times* article, "The Case for Contamination": "Cultures are made of continuities and changes, and the identity of a society can survive through these changes. Societies without change aren't authentic; they're just dead."[3]

Better to concentrate the efforts of the public schools on the most urgent need: helping these children acquire the language of the majority society for equal educational and employment opportunities, and for becoming socially engaged with classmates and the community—as rapidly as possible. One Mexican American professor of literature spoke eloquently of his transformation in an elementary school classroom when he acquired the common language:

One day in school I raised my hand to volunteer an answer. I spoke out in a loud voice. And I did not think it remarkable when the entire class understood. That day, I moved far from the disadvantaged child I had been only days earlier. . . . I had a public identity. Only later when I was able to think of myself as an American, no longer an alien in gringo society, could I seek the rights and opportunities for full public individuality. . . . Those middle class ethnics who scorn assimilation, romanticize public separateness, and they trivialize the dilemma of the socially disadvantaged.[4]

Indeed, Richard Rodriguez grew up to become a professor of English literature with a focus on the works of Shakespeare.

The City of Newton, Massachusetts, with one of the most high-achieving public school systems in the country, encouraged language and culture maintenance outside the school day. An after-school Italian language and culture program for children in grades 1–6 met twice weekly; a mini-course for Spanish speakers was offered after school as well. Community groups sponsored their own efforts including Saturday morning lessons in Japanese, Chinese, and Hebrew cultures. These voluntary programs relied on the priorities of students and their parents, not on state mandates.

A grave national misunderstanding about non-English-speaking children was finally addressed in the 1980s and 1990s. Historically, immigrants from southern and eastern Europe migrating in large numbers in the late nineteenth and early twentieth centuries were popularly considered to be of low mental capacity. For the children, there were no special lessons in the school day for quickly mastering the English language, and they were sometimes labeled "EMR," educably mentally retarded.

As a result of our far more enlightened times, after the 1960s, solid investments from federal and state sources support special help. Three federal programs were designed for their needs: Title I for children of poverty who are below grade level in reading and math; Special Education for children with learning disabilities; and Bilingual Education for non-English speakers.

As the director of the Bilingual/English as a Second Language programs in the Newton, Massachusetts, public schools, it soon became clear to me that the distinctions between programs were a contentious issue. One day, at a meeting of administrators, it was announced that since bilingual students are educationally disadvantaged, they should come under the special education umbrella. I objected forcefully to such a designation. It was urgent to inform the group of administrators that making such a change would be the most demoralizing action for everyone—students, parents, and teachers.

Across the country, professionals work mightily now to make everyone recognize that bilingual children are not mentally retarded or disabled. They are only temporarily lacking in a sufficient knowledge of English, a situation that is remedied in a few months or a year or two. Newton officials, to their credit, understood the reasoning and did not change the education of our English language learners, the latest official label for these students.

Thirty years of the bold experiment proved bilingual programs fail to meet the goals of the legislation: students do not learn English more rapidly for regular classroom work, do not learn subject matter better when taught in their native language, and do not have higher "self-esteem" from having their family language used in the classroom.[5]

Antonio Gramsci, Italian anarchist and fiery revolutionary in the early twentieth century, is an odd choice to quote, but he spoke well on the subject of knowing one's national, standard language:

> Someone who only speaks dialect, or understands the standard language incompletely, necessarily has an intuition of the world which is more or less limited and provincial . . . without the mastery of the common standard version of the national language, one is inevitably destined to function at the periphery of national life, and especially, outside the national and political mainstream.[6]

VOTING IN TWO LANGUAGES

Meanwhile, back at the multicultural ranch, the 1975 extension of the original Voting Rights Act created a new government obligation: voting information services and ballots must now be provided in two languages if a district includes 5 percent or more eligible voters who speak a language other than English. This federal mandate imposes an expensive obligation on local districts. Two questions arise: how is the 5 percent determined, and why do this at all?

The Bureau of the Census answers the first question. The bureau asks people who say they speak another language at home to answer if they speak English "very well," "well," "poorly," or "not at all." Incredible as it may seem, all those who answer "well," "poorly," or "not at all" are assumed to need a voting ballot in their native language. It is reasonable to ask why people who state that they speak English "well" would need an accommodation in their first language?

As to the "why" part, since it has been federal law since 1907 that naturalized citizens must demonstrate the ability to read, write, and speak English, who are the people for whom a bilingual ballot is necessary? This accommodation for new citizens makes no sense at all. Naturalized immigrants must reside in the United States for five years and pass a citizenship test administered in English in order to become U.S. citizens, and thus be eligible to vote.

The original reason for bilingual ballots was not meant for all immigrants but for resident groups that were deemed to have had inferior access to educational opportunities, that is, Native Americans, Hispanic Americans, and Asian Americans.

This unfunded federal mandate is expensive enough, for instance, when ten counties in Florida must provide Spanish-language ballots, but what of the expense to districts in California where voting materials must be provided in four to six other languages such as Chinese, Korean, Filipino, and Vietnamese? In a recent election, Los Angeles County, for example, spent $3.3 million to provide multilingual ballots.[7]

The divisive effects of this ill-begotten initiative encourage the maintenance of separate enclaves, resistance to the mastering of the common language of the nation, and creating obstacles to a unifying culture. Under the 1965 Voting Rights Act, all voters have the right to bring a helper into the polls, an interpreter if they do not understand the language, a reader if they cannot read or have some other disability.

Hard to believe, but the U.S. Justice Department actually decided in 2007 that it was not enough for Boston to have voting materials printed in Mandarin, Cantonese, and English, but that even the *names* on the ballot must be translated for the Chinese community. Because the writing of names in the Chinese dialects is phonetic, finding characters that closely match the sound of each syllable results in an enormous probability of error.

Massachusetts Attorney General William Galvin rejected the edict from Washington. He offered the evidence that the name of Governor Mitt Romney would appear as *Sticky Rice* or *Uncooked Rice*; Mayor Tom Menino's name would appear as *Imbecile* or *Rainbow Farmer*. Galvin declared this transliteration of names would cause chaos and have no effect on reducing fraud.[8]

OVERTURNING BILINGUAL EDUCATION BY POPULAR VOTE

From the 1980s on, research studies documented the failure of bilingual education programs, but state governors and state legislatures, annually, failed to take the lead in initiating changes in state laws. It was up to groups of citizens to begin demanding the removal of bilingual programs and their replacement with intensive English language teaching.

The revolt started in California, the state with the largest proportion of "English Language Learners" in the United States. One in every four public school students in California starts school without a sufficient knowledge of the English language to be able to learn school subjects taught in English. These children need special help, instruction in the English language, to make the most of educational opportunities and to become a part of their school and community.

In California, the Question 227 referendum, "English for the Children," received 60 percent of the popular vote in the 1998 election, in spite of a lavishly financed campaign against it led by the Spanish-language TV network Univision. The California Teachers Union also campaigned against the referendum, as did leaders of both political parties and the governor.

Funding to pay for collecting signatures to put the question on the ballot came from Ron K. Unz, a successful Silicon Valley entrepreneur and political activist. He understood the plight of immigrant children as he had been brought to the United States from Germany as a young child.

Twenty-five years of damaging, separate "bilingual" teaching was finally nullified. California reports its students are learning English rapidly, demonstrating better performance annually on state tests of reading, writing, and math in English since the change in the law.[9]

In Arizona, the state on the Mexican border with a high proportion of Spanish speakers, a similar referendum campaign was waged in 2000, with an even higher percentage of success. Sixty-two percent of Arizona voters favored "English for the Children." In Arizona as in California, Ron K. Unz supported the referendum. Arizona, too, has reported documented academic improvements for "English Learners" since the change in the law.[10]

THE MASSACHUSETTS CAMPAIGN
DEFIES THE COMMON WISDOM

On to Massachusetts with "English for the Children," where I reluctantly agreed to co-chair the state campaign. In this most liberal of all the fifty states, one might reasonably fear defeat for such an initiative. Once again Mr. Unz funded the signature gathering and contributed his expertise in public relations.

Three activists led the Massachusetts English for the Children campaign. Between them, they touched all the politically correct bases: Lincoln Tamayo, attorney and administrator at Boston University (a Latino); Christine M. Rossell, head of the political science department at Boston University (an egghead); and Rosalie Porter (an immigrant). As in California and Arizona, both major political parties opposed the campaign, as did the teachers' unions, the National Education Association, and the American Federation of Teachers.

But here, for the first time, a candidate for public office supported "English for the Children"—Mitt Romney, who was running for governor. He declared publicly that children should be given special help to learn English from the very first day of school, to make the best use of educational opportunities in our country. Massachusetts voters, to their credit, voted 68 percent in favor of throwing out the state Transitional Bilingual Education Act of 1971.

The new law mandating English immersion teaching was challenged in California in federal court and upheld as constitutionally correct. Only Alaska, Illinois, New Jersey, and Texas still retain their bilingual education mandates. Initiative and referenda are not allowed in New Jersey and Texas and, although permitted in Illinois, the process is so difficult that it is effectively moot there. Citizen activists can succeed in overturning unjust laws, but it takes decades of hard work, adequate funding, and seriously dedicated activists to make it happen.[11]

The obvious benefits to immigrant children of learning English as quickly as possible should be apparent for what is now labeled "inclusion" but was once called "assimilation." The "A" word is now totally out of favor, not to be spoken in polite society.

In an August 2021 letter to supporters, ProEnglish executive director Stephen Guschov stated, "Immigrants who learn the common language of the country they are living in 'are more likely to assimilate and become self-sufficient, no longer needing government assistance.' Through the assimilation of earlier immigrants over succeeding generations, the USA became the most successful multiethnic nation in world history."

DRIVING IN TWO LANGUAGES: AN EXPENSIVE, MISGUIDED FEDERAL IMPOSITION

A related development to bilingual ballots is the practice of having driver's license tests and preparatory materials translated into several languages. Each state has the responsibility of crafting its own laws governing the issuing of driver's licenses. The imposition of this burden is an expansion of the 1964 Civil Rights Act that has not yet been challenged in court.

In 2021, thirty-two states have official English laws in place, that is, the language of official government business in these states must be conducted in English. Yet these official English laws have not prevented the driver's license test from being prepared for and administered in a number of other languages.

Alabama is a good case in point. The state incurs the expense of having all preparatory materials and the driver's test translated into these languages: Arabic, Chinese, French, German, Greek, Japanese, Korean, Russian, Spanish, Thai, and Vietnamese.

A challenge to this practice was brought against Alabama by attorneys for the Pro-English organization in Washington, DC, in 2007. The main argument was that giving the exam in multiple languages violated a constitutional amendment that designates English as Alabama's official language. In the 1990 election, Alabama voters by a 9–1 margin had approved a change in the state constitution to require that the state shall make no law diminishing the role of English as the common language of the state of Alabama, and that the state legislature shall enforce this amendment.

Yet despite the clear language in this amendment, the Alabama Supreme Court voted 5–4 to reject the argument against multilanguage driver's tests. Chief Justice Sue Bell Cobb reasoned that allowing people with limited English to take the test in their native language helped them get a license, become assimilated, and increase their access to education, employment, and shopping.[12] Mobility is not necessarily language enhancing. The ability to drive a car does not promote the learning of English, as the court seems to proclaim, though it will surely help with shopping.

In 2008, the Southeastern Legal Foundation brought a similar suit against the Alabama language policy in Montgomery County, and again it was dismissed. My involvement in this case as an expert witness for the Southeastern Legal Foundation lawsuit spurred my original interest in the driver's license test issue.

Considering the costs to Alabama taxpayers of drivers' tests in twelve languages besides English, an examination of the population figures at the time of the lawsuit is revealing. In the 2000 census, the state reported 3,990,000 residents speak English well, out of a population of 4,152,000. For the Alabama Department of Public Safety to provide these multilingual services for just two percent of the population may be seen as an elite extravagance or an unjustifiable waste of public money. To date it has not been possible to obtain actual cost figures from the state.

Another question that the state has been reluctant to answer, if they even keep such records, is how many people applying for driver's licenses actually request and use the translated materials? How many Thai speakers? Speakers of Arabic, of German?

Besides the obvious safety issue of licensed drivers in Alabama who cannot read or understand road signs, and the costs to taxpayers, this state law has another negative effect. It weakens a new immigrant's impulse to master the English language quickly for educational and employment opportunities as well as the benefit of acquiring a driver's license.

Last item on the subject: advocates for multilingual driver's license tests claim that states not allowing the use of other languages would lose federal transportation funds over the language issue. This threat has no legal validity, and none of the nine states that offer driver's license tests only in English have yet lost federal funds because of the language of their drivers' tests.[13]

DAMAGE DONE: BEYOND EDUCATION

Two generations of American students have been nurtured on the multi-culturalist/diversity concept, being taught the equality of all cultures as a non-negotiable ideal. All groups are expected to achieve at equal rates and be proportionately represented in every institution of public life.

This is a fallacy, of course, but it has encouraged the rewriting of school textbooks to present a historical view in which every group is equally recognized for something, while the role of the founders and historical leaders of our country (dead White males) is greatly diminished, if their history is still taught much at all.

Higher education has enormously enlarged this preoccupation with the proliferation of victims' studies departments for all minorities on college campuses. The "diversity" agenda denies individual differences of intellectual, religious, political, or artistic capacities, attitudes, or beliefs, and deems skin color and ancestors' national origins as the principal defining elements of groups of human beings.

In 2022, in fact, in view of the current state of higher education, with tuition and fees having climbed inexorably every year, outstripping the rise in the cost of living, one may well ask what exactly is the mission of colleges. Is higher education now only a vehicle for promoting politically progressive ideology and not for developing academic excellence?

There is a demand for ever-growing numbers of "under-represented" groups to be preferred—women (who actually comprise 60 percent of college students earning bachelor degrees), gays, Latinos, Blacks, whatever. What should we think when the University of Massachusetts announced in the late 1990s that 18 percent of its students were African American, but this group made up less than 11 percent of Massachusetts residents? Would the university have reduced the percentage of African American students to conform to the correct degree of "diversity?" Of course not.

One of the most highly rated liberal arts colleges in the United States, Amherst College, is, like almost all of higher education, obsessed with racism. In March 2020, President Biddy Martin addressed a statement to the college community, published in the student newspaper, frankly admitting that "we have not done all we can to create an environment that is truly inclusive and free from racism."

Apparently, the college had mistreated its minority students on issues of race. Her *mea culpa*, accepting responsibility and promising urgent new initiatives to improve it all, will almost certainly result in investments in more "woke" programs and administrators to address past iniquities.[14]

In 2021, Amherst College, celebrated the 200th year of it's founding in 1821. The college reported an incredible new fact: the massive improvement in the composition of its student body, is described thus: "a school once known as a bastion of wealthy, white (and for over 150 years, male) students has an incoming class this year in which about 51percent of the U.S. students identify as people of color."[15]

Multiculturalism/diversity, the underpinnings for racial preference legislation, has prevailed for decades. The notion of individual preference or choice is superseded by considerations of group identity. The widespread acceptance of civil rights for all Americans is not in question, uniformly strengthened since Martin Luther King, Jr., fought and died for its realization. His highest hope for America was respect and tolerance for all of us united "in a single garment of destiny."[16]

But the "diversity" concept is diametrically opposed to King's ideals and America's genius as a nation. Supreme Court Justice Powell first pronounced "diversity" as a compelling interest in the 1978 *Bakke* case challenge to affirmative action.[17] The concept was reaffirmed in the 2003 *Grutter* decision when Justice Sandra Day O'Connor wrote that the temporary "diversity" rationale of 1978 must not extend for more than twenty-five years.[18]

The true agenda of multiculturalism/diversity favors racial and ethnic discrimination to achieve a predetermined demographic mix while opposing merit and assimilation to American culture, a static rather than dynamic view of society.

The U.S. Supreme Court announced that it would hear a case involving race-conscious admissions at the University of Texas in the fall session of 2012 (*Fisher v. University of Texas*).[19] The university argued for continuing to use race in its admissions policy because of the educational benefits of "diversity." Ms. Fisher, who was denied admission, sued the university to challenge that policy.

The crux of the matter is this: the high court held for the first time in the 2003 *Grutter* decision that "racial diversity in higher education qualifies as a compelling governmental interest. *Such a state interest is essential when a government classifies individuals by race*" (author's emphasis).[20]

This statement raises this basic question: *Why must we continue to be classified by race?* The Fisher decision in 2016 was a narrow ruling; again the Supreme Court justices evaded the challenge of deciding once and for all to end the affirmative action law that has outlived its effectiveness.

Chapter 2

HARVARD UNIVERSITY BROUGHT TO TASK

In 2019 a lawsuit was filed against Harvard University by Students for Fair Admissions, a group representing Asian American students. Their claim is that Harvard's use of race favors Blacks, Latinx (a new designation to avoid using the proper "Latino" or "Latina" word that is correct in Spanish-language grammar), and Whites at the expense of Asian Americans.

A district court judge ruled that even if Asian Americans are penalized, it is justified due to the compelling interest in diversity that benefits a college population. In November 2020, the First Circuit Court agreed, supporting Harvard's admissions policy as consistent with Supreme Court precedent.[21]

The Harvard case has been appealed to the Supreme Court and a sea change has occurred there since the Fisher case was heard. Three new justices who lean conservative have been appointed. On Monday, January 24, 2022, the Supreme Court announced that it will rule on the use of race-conscious college admissions in the next year's session. It will consider challenges to student admission policies at Harvard University and the University of North Carolina.[22]

It may be that the Supreme Court will finally end the four decades of race-based college admissions in the name of the "D" word. There is reason for optimism and hope that in 2023 the court will finally issue a definitive ruling that ends racial preferences—an event devoutly to be desired, at least by this writer. Even with a conservative majority on the court, the Supreme Court justices may still be reluctant to resolve this issue with a definitive ruling. A substantial amount of courage is on order.

AN INSPIRING VOTE IN THE 2020 ELECTION IN CALIFORNIA

A noteworthy event occurred in the November 3, 2020, election. A referendum question on the California ballot, Proposition 16, asked voters to reject Proposition 209, the 1996 referendum measure that says: "the state cannot discriminate or grant preferential treatment based on race, sex, color, ethnicity, or national origin in public accommodations, admissions, or contracting."[23]

California has the most ethnically varied population in the country, yet the people voted by 57 percent to 42 percent not to bring back racial preferences. That is an amazing outcome, which mirrors the documented fact that Americans across the country—of whatever political persuasion—do not favor preferences for any group. Time for the justices to step up to the plate and hit a home run on this issue.

LAST CONSIDERATIONS

It is past time that we consider some attitudinal changes in these related areas:

- It is time to encourage assimilation by helping newcomers enter the larger U.S. society by learning the majority language, or are we bound to continue promoting ethnic and linguistic separatism in the name of multiculturalism?
- It is time to stop spending public funds to enforce ethnic/racial/gender identity propaganda in K–12 schools, leaving these activities to family and community initiatives outside of the school day, and focus again on teaching basic school subjects.
- It is time to stop trying to preserve 322 languages through our public schools but focus instead on giving immigrant students the essential skills in English to give them social and academic achievement opportunities.
- It is time we, as a country, get well beyond artificial divisions of racial and ancestry labels, the "diversity"-inspired spoils system, that is hurting our national unity.

Let us hope for a turn in a better direction very soon to undo the damage of diversity politics.

NOTES

1. Rosalie Pedalino Porter. *Forked Tongue: The Politics of Bilingual Education* (New Jersey: Transaction Publishers, 1996).

2. "Bilingual Education v. English Immersion," *Congressional Quarterly Researcher*, Volume 19, Number 43 (December 2009): http://www.sagepub.com/healeyregc6e/study/chapter/cq/87318_02.pdf.

3. Kwame Anthony Appiah, "The Case for Contamination," *The New York Times*, January 1, 2006: https://www.nytimes.com/2006/01/01/magazine/the-case-for-contamination.html.

4. Richard Rodriguez, *Hunger of Memories: The Education of Richard Rodriguez* (Boston: David R Godine, 1982), 22.

5. Rosalie Pedalino Porter, "Selected Studies" (Fact Sheet, 2009).

6. Antonio Gramsci, *Letters from Prison* (New York: Columbia University Press, 1994), 325.

7. Stephen Guschov, "Non-English Ballots In 29 States in 2018," *ProEnglish*, January 4, 2018: https://proenglish.org/2018/01/04/non-english-ballots-in-29-states-in-2018/.

8. Frank Phillips, "Ballot translations could mean too much," *The Boston Globe,* June 26, 2007.

9. Joanne Jacobs, "The Education of JAIME CAPELLAN: English Learner Success in California Schools," *Lexington Institute,* June 17, 2008: https://www .lexingtoninstitute.org/the-education-of-jaime-capellan-english-learner-success-in -california-schools/.

10. Rosalie Pedalino Porter, "Nogales Unified School District and State of Arizona Programs for English Language Learners (ELL)," expert report in *Flores v. State of Arizona,* 2010.

11. *Valeria G. et al. v. State of California,* "A Challenge to the Legality of Proposition 227, English for the Children," July 15, 1998.

12. Phillip Rawls, "Ala. Court Backs Exam in Multiple Languages," Associated Press, October 20, 2007.

13. ProEnglish data available at http://www.ProEnglish.org.

14. Biddy Martin, "Statement on Addressing Racism on Campus," *The Amherst Student,* March 27, 2020.

15. Pfarrer, Steve, "200 Years of Learning: Amherst College History Marked by Growth and Change," *Daily Hampshire Gazette,* August 4, 2021.

16. Clegg, Roger, "Attacking 'Diversity': A Review of Peter Wood's *Diversity: The Invention of Concept,*" *Journal of College and University Law* 31, no. 2, 2005.

17. *Regents of the University of California v. Bakke,* 438 U.S. 265 (1978).

18. *Grutter v. Bollinger,* 539 U.S. 306, 343 (2003).

19. *Fisher v. University of Texas* (2010): http://thf_media.s3.amazonaws.com/2011 /pdf/PLF_CEO_ACRI_P21_Amicus_Brief.pdf.

20. Jess Bravin, "Justices to Revisit Race-Based Admissions," *Wall Street Journal,* February 22, 2012.

21. Bianca Quinlan, "Appeals Court Rules in Favor of Harvard in Affirmation Action Case, Paving Way for Supreme Court Challenge," *Politico Education,* November 12, 2020.

22. Brent Kendall and Melissa Korn, "High Court to Hear Admissions Cases," *Wall Street Journal,* January 25, 2022, A3.

23. Jessica Wolf and Melissa Abraham, "Prop 16 Failed in California. Why? And What's next?," *UCLA Newsroom,* November 18, 2020: https://newsroom.ucla.edu/ stories/prop-16-failed-in-california.

3

Identity Politics Is the New Spoils System

The Imposition of Color, National Origins, Gender, and Sexual Personae as Group Dividers and Victim Creators

The Civil Rights Act of 1964 and the Voting Rights Act of 1965 are the magnificent legislative achievements that began an era of substantially strengthening the goal of prohibiting racial discrimination. At that time and as is the case today, the mainstream press did not much emphasize the fact that both of those bills were passed with a majority of Republican votes. In fact, Republicans in both houses of Congress voted for the bills with higher percentages than did the Democrats. Our Democrat President Lyndon Johnson justly received the credit. Preeminent sociologists of that era, Daniel Patrick Moynihan and Nathan Glazer, authors of *Beyond the Melting Pot* (1963) had an early influence in defining group characteristics in the U.S. population of immigrant descendants.

The first government-mandated initiative to collect data on groups in the United States was in 1966, the work of the Equal Employment Opportunity Commission (EEOC), which proposed four types of disadvantaged groups to account for: Negro, American Indian, Oriental, and Spanish-surnamed. Ah, the innocence of these quaintly antique labels. The original intent was to tabulate their numbers and to determine how each group's presence was represented in schools, in private and public sector employment, and to gauge if that number was consistent with their percentage of the U.S. population.

Yet, at the very beginning of this whole endeavor of classifying Americans, hardly anyone questioned the validity of the new category "Spanish-surnamed." Why lump together people who identified originally from thirty-five different Spanish-speaking countries and declare them all "disadvantaged"? Where was the rationality in this? Well, it soon became clear. This sorting of a disparate group of Americans of Spanish-speaking backgrounds into one category would create a large enough group to wield serious political power.

The early categories were standardized in 1977 by the Office of Management and Budget (OMB) as follows: White, Black, Hispanic, Asian, and American Indian/Alaska Native. Special victim status was now conferred on these last four categories, thanks to lobbying by liberal advocacy groups. In fact, the word "Hispanic" was created out of thin air to justify this artificial group.

The whole enterprise is so expansive that it diluted the fine goal of removing racial discrimination from the lives of the descendants of those who suffered the original sin of slavery. Illogical and inaccurate, it categorized people from various countries, tribes, backgrounds into groups deserving preferences. It boggles the mind, but it became the basis for Affirmative Action legislation. That "temporary" law to redress inequality became a thriving government industry that, fifty years later and, in spite of several limiting rulings by the U.S. Supreme Court, firmly resists its own demise.

In the 1980s, the U.S. Census began counting the whole country under these five labels—white, black, brown, yellow, and red—supposedly to match the OMB designations. Also, a further refinement in that "Hispanic" category—one could identify as Hispanic/White or Hispanic/Black. And thus it remains to this day. How has it changed our country? Immensely. We are a country divided into five separate official groups, four of which are widely known to deserve all manner of preferences and one that is understood to be the villainous perpetrator of all bad acts of discrimination. An accepted practice of "bean counting" and blaming permeates every aspect of public life.

From the mid-1970s until now, observing the identity spoils system phenomenon in public education has been my professional work as a teacher, administrator, researcher, and public advocate for immigrant children.

The United States started as a country that received immigrants, not always with open arms. The expectation was that with time and each new generation, immigrants would adapt to the culture of their new land. Instead, half a century ago we began to make a fetish of "differences," encouraging immigrants to preserve their languages and cultures as if by divine right, dismissing assimilation as evil. Victor Davis Hanson aptly and succinctly sums up the new view: "Difference was now no longer a necessary prelude to assimilation but a desirable, permanent and separate tribalism."[1]

My observations of the effects of this ethos in educational settings is demonstrated in a few appropriate examples.

IN THE EARLY YEARS OF SCHOOLING

In a 1976 directive to the elementary schools in the Commonwealth of Massachusetts, teachers were informed of the rules for identifying young students showing above-average academic promise, to enroll these children in gifted and talented programs. These prestigious new programs were exciting as they offered more advanced lessons for students who learned more rapidly than their classmates in the core subjects of reading, writing, math, and science.

However, there was one caveat: every school must take care that the children selected for gifted and talented programs reflect the racial make-up of the school. When a teacher tactfully mentioned that there might not be exactly that number of qualified students from each racial group who showed above-average academic promise, one school principal remarked, "Then think up some other characteristics, like 'leadership' or 'congeniality' to justify the selection." That was four-and-a-half decades ago.

AN EXEMPLARY PUBLIC CHARTER SCHOOL

In this year of 2021, "bean counting" and manipulating population data is common in elementary schools. The Pioneer Valley Chinese Immersion Charter School (PVCICS) in Hadley, Massachusetts, provides a useful example. It is a unique school founded with the precise goal of providing intensive instruction in Mandarin Chinese, several hours a day, for students in kindergarten through grade 12.

Over a dozen years, the school has proven that American children are capable of mastering fluency and literacy in a second language to a high level, as well as scoring high grades on their regular schoolwork in English. Most recently, in April 2021, the school was recognized as the highest-performing charter school as well as the second-highest-performing high school in Massachusetts on student scores in reading and math—in English.[2]

Is this not a record of excellence to be lauded by state education authorities? Well, yes, but then our bureaucratic masters raise an odd question with the school every year: why do you not have a higher proportion of English-language learners in your school? The school administrators do not dare answer with a logical statement such as this: why would an immigrant family with children who do not know English want to enroll them in a school where all the children are learning Chinese?

The Chinese Immersion Charter School enrolls students of every racial and ethnic variety, but state officials still oblige them to try to recruit children who would not find the school suitable. The first priority for the families of immigrant children, stated to me hundreds of times in my teaching years, was that their children be taught the language of the classroom and the community—English. Why is this simple, sensible idea not readily understood by the state bureaucrats?

In the example from the Pioneer Valley Chinese Immersion Charter School, one begins to understand how identity politics has been employed to impose a quota system. The basic fallacy on which it is based is the notion that in an open democracy such as ours, the only proof of a fair society is to find that in every job, career, profession, school, and social group the five designated groups are represented according to their percentages in the population. But will 51 percent of all women want to be engineers or physicists or crane operators? Will 12 percent of all CPAs and Spanish teachers be African American?

AT THE COLLEGE AND UNIVERSITY LEVEL: RESEGREGATION AND ITS DISCONTENTS

At the college and university level, high dropout rates are routinely documented at elite institutions that recruit academically unqualified students in order to reach their racial/ethnic quotas. It is commonly known but rarely announced that this practice harms minority students who could well succeed at less prestigious schools. It is unacceptable to speak the blasphemous word "quotas," but in reality, that is what affirmative action goals represent. Or, one might employ the term sociologist Nathan Glazer created for this situation in the title of one of his books, *Affirmative Discrimination*, the denying of acceptance to qualified applicants in favor of admitting those racially and ethnically "kosher."

There is a strong impulse among college administrators to suppress any evidence of poor outcomes where affirmative action is concerned. Professor Amy Wax at the University of Pennsylvania Law School suffered the ignominy of being scolded publicly by some students and faculty. Her sin was the reporting of data showing that students admitted under preferences are less academically qualified and have very high dropout rates.

The law school dean demanded she take a year's leave and forbade her from teaching freshmen courses. However, that was not punishment enough. The local head of Black Lives Matter Pennsylvania demanded that she be fired immediately or there would be consequences on the campus. It is dangerous to speak uncomfortable truths in a university setting.[3]

The excoriating of professor Amy Wax continues as new instances of apostasy discovered in her earlier work have caused much virtue signaling and supposed shock around the academic globe. A single consolation for Professor Wax may be her public recognition in April 2018, when she was awarded the prestigious Academic Courage Award by *The American Scholar*.

What became of our glorious movement from the 1960s of promoting societal integration, to be fostered in communities and schools? By the late 1970s, early 1980s, campus dorms were gradually moving away from the aim of assigning students of different backgrounds to shared living space. The resegregation of the college campus began, catering to the new demands for dorms and social clubs matching certain identities, that is, New Africa House, Asia House, Casa Latina.

In an interview at Oberlin College, a Japanese American freshman student was asked if she would choose her favored dorm to match her ethnic identity. Her answer was "No, I don't see myself as only Asian-American, there's so much more to me than just that designation."[4]

At Hamilton College in upstate New York, president Eugene Tobin announced a new initiative he called a *posse* movement, the idea that minority students should be grouped with their like in dorms, preferably with applicants who came from their same neighborhood or city, so that they would feel at home. The word "tribes" was used in connection with the *posse* idea.

The program expanded over the years to Posse Boston and Posse Miami, until 2018 when the Boston group was eliminated, with fumbling but incoherent excuses for the change. One idea that Hamilton *bien-pensant* administrators will not acknowledge or discuss is the reality that minority students are having difficulty keeping up with studies. But the college vaunts the fact that 40 percent of their current enrollment are "minority students."[5]

But didn't we once consider college as the time to be living among a variety of people not from your own neighborhood? Is this not the time in a young person's development where it is beneficial to mingle with and come to know and understand people quite different from oneself? That notion, I'm afraid, bit the dust, greatly overshadowed by the favored impulse to remain with one's group, unless that group happens to be a fraternity.

Not only are students encouraged to be one with their own racial/ethnic/sexual group, but they must loudly denounce anyone on campus who dares to misappropriate another's cultural symbols, clothing, foods, whatever. No more wearing Indian feather headdresses, Mexican sombreros, or the like, to a Halloween party, or to be seen to favor Thai or other exotic foods—no, no, this is now a racist display.

How many more minor aggressions can be created by our privileged young students in highly respected schools to allow them to outdo one another in their self-depiction as victims, the new *desideratum*? Hence, the birth of intersectionality.

THE SIN OF CULTURAL APPROPRIATION

On the Yale campus in November 2015, a hapless young faculty member dared question the wisdom of having the college impose rules on what kind of Halloween costumes should be allowed on campus. Erika Christakis, a specialist in early childhood education, challenged students to stand up for their right to decide how to dress up for Halloween, saying in part, "Is there no room anymore for a child or young person to be a little bit obnoxious or provocative or, yes, offensive?"

The reaction to that email was instant and physically frightening. Not only was the now despised "white woman" shouted at with accusations and obscenities at her own home, but she and her husband were soon made so unwelcome that they resigned their positions.

How did Yale University, that august establishment for educating "the great and the good," follow up on the vicious behavior of students? The African American woman who led the attack on Christakis home was honored at the following year's commencement ceremony. Imagine the roles of attacker and attacked to be reversed, and the public outcry would have been heard on Mars.[6]

In the winter of 2020, the Palm Beach Convention Center Theater advertised an upcoming performance of the musical *Hamilton*, the new work of Puerto Rican musical creator Lin-Manuel Miranda. This magnificent portrayal of the founding of our country by the usual gang of Jefferson, Madison, Washington, and others had every character portrayed by an African American actor.

It is a musical work of genius worthy of its success, but does no one notice that there is a large amount of cultural appropriation going on here? To date, no word of criticism has appeared in theater reviews. Why not? Ah, perhaps one should understand that it is only mandatory to complain when a person of "whiteness" takes on a character part or an item of clothing or a food of some other culture.

LITERARY CROSS OVER

Have noted Black writers of the past five decades routinely denounced writers of other ethnicities for writing about Blacks? Today in our feverishly ramped up *wokeness*, one would probably not find a Black writer defending racial crossover in literature. In 1968 a group of Black writers convened to express their disapproval of William Styron for publishing *The Confessions of Nat Turner*. That a White writer would presume to write a first-person narrative of a Black rebel leader was strongly criticized. All Black writers did not agree with this thinking.[7]

One of the greatest American writers of the second half of the twentieth century, James Baldwin, was a strong defender of racial crossover in literature and in life. In the early 1980s, Baldwin was on the faculty at the University of Massachusetts in Amherst. Baldwin said of Styron's controversial Nat Turner book, "He has begun the common history . . . [o]urs." Baldwin never changed his mind about the value of what Styron had done.[8]

It is puzzling today that the late Baldwin is revered as a hero of the Black Lives Matter movement when some of his major works, *Giovanni's Room* and *Another Country*, were almost entirely peopled by White characters. Until his death in 1984, Baldwin socialized and enjoyed close friendships with Whites, behavior not much tolerated today. It would certainly not be acknowledged or honored by the Black Lives Matter group.

A quarter century after Baldwin's defense of Styron, Toni Morrison was asked if she thought Styron had the right to publish a book about Nat Turner. She said, "Of course he does. He has the right to write about whatever he wants. To suggest otherwise is outrageous." In 2021, even such a universally recognized Black author as Toni Morrison might be "cancelled" for such heresy.[9]

In his 1962 article, "Letter from a Region in My Mind," Baldwin gave us a magnificent statement that should rightfully inspire us today:

> For the sake of one's children, in order to minimize the bill that they must pay, one must be careful not to take refuge in any delusion, and the value placed on the color of the skin is always and everywhere and forever a delusion. . . . I know that what I am asking is impossible. But in our time, as in every time, the impossible is the least that one can demand. (104)

Many do not accept today's insistence on the Black/White binary, that skin color is the most important element distinguishing human beings. Today the high priest of the new anti-racism, Ibram X. Kendi (*How to Be an Anti-Racist*, 2020) sets forth a bold statement on the correct posture for our times, a statement that is so often quoted that it hardly needs attribution: "The only remedy to past discrimination is present discrimination. The only remedy to present discrimination is future discrimination." That would certainly confirm that Professor Kendi is not shy about promoting unending racial strife.[10]

Literary crossover is not limited to Black/White subjects alone. For whatever reason, several decades ago people were not squeamish about attending a theater or movie performance that presented an artistic work created by a person not of the same ethnicity as the characters in the play. As one example, a hit play on Broadway in 1955 was *A View from the Bridge*, a tragic drama exploring the tensions in an Italian American Brooklyn family where incestuous lust and jealousy are on display. The play was a great Broadway success, and there was never a word of the fact that Arthur Miller, a Jew, was writing about Italians.

Another example of the lack of negative commentary is Irving Berlin's composing the best-loved songs for Christian religious holidays, *White Christmas* and *Easter Parade*. That a Jewish song writer created songs that seem never to lose their popularity was not a subject for public criticism. Would Irving Berlin be "cancelled" today for creating a song with "White" in the title and lyrics that surely must be seen as a microaggression, bad enough to require that all his songs be "disappeared"?

These examples of crossover are few and obvious. The subject deserves serious research to trace, with sufficient data and examples, how and when the downgrading of crossover in literature developed. A doctoral thesis on the subject for aspiring current scholars will interest and enlighten us all.

BACK TO THE MELTING POT

Returning to the seminal sociological study of immigrant groups by Moynihan and Glazer, *Beyond the Melting Pot: The Negroes, Puerto Ricans, Jews, Italians and Irish of New York City.* (1970) is instructive. One of the important lessons Glazer and Moynihan reported was that over time and succeeding generations, the people in these immigrant groups learned to share and celebrate each other's differences.

Over three generations, people in each of these groups came together, with a growing understanding of each other's individual characteristics through school and work experiences and through intergroup marriage. That is how immigrants were expected to grow in confidence in their new country and learn to appreciate and accept differences.

COMMENCEMENTS SEGREGATED: BY CHOICE

To the *ne plus ultra* of elitism, a look at Harvard University's 2017 commencement illustrates the new nature of cap-and-gown activities. They hosted their first ceremony segregated by skin color. In addition to the regular graduate department ceremonies, there was a Black commencement, a celebration of the "Black Diaspora at Harvard" as it was termed by one of the speakers.[11]

Let's parse the meaning here: privileged students attending Harvard while Black, hold their own ceremony to denigrate their non-black classmates and to claim continuing victimhood. That's quite a trick. Some in our society who were not privileged to attend college after high school due to family poverty would be ecstatic to put up with a little discomfort at Harvard—or even at East Podunk U.

But it is not only Black diaspora students at Harvard who are treated to a separate ceremony. For the third year in a row, Harvard hosted a ceremony for Latino students called the LatinX Event; the University of Delaware hosts a "Lavender" graduation for LGBTQ students; and Columbia University offers a separate ceremony for students who are first in their families to earn a college degree.

It is time to consider the "intersectionality" craze. It is the new normal to boast of being victimized in several different categories, as the grievance industry grinds on. The potential for an increasing number of separate ceremonies dazzles the mind—why not individual graduation ceremonies for sexual abuse survivors, for adoptees, for Muslims, Asians, physically handicapped students? Would that a college administrator might be brave enough to say, "Hey, folks, let's go back to reality and have just one commencement for all."[12]

STEM AND WOMEN'S CHOICES

Why don't more women choose careers in science, technology, engineering and math (STEM)? This provocative question is often raised by culture warriors as one more example of the unfairness of our society. Apparently, feminists have come to believe almost universally that real equity will be achieved when women fill 50 percent or more of the positions in every profession where men have been a recognizable majority. Some may find this notion ludicrous, but it is only the latest example of using thinly disguised quotas as the yardstick of access.

Women in the United States have the capacity to enter any profession and pursue it to its highest levels, given the ambition to work, study, and adapt one's personal choices to fit the needed requirements. Of course, there is timing and good health and a little luck involved, for women as for men.

Data collection and analysis on this gender question provides us with some unanticipated answers. The study published recently in the journal *Psychological Science* examines the results of the PISA (Program for International Student Assessment), the largest skills test of fifteen-year-olds that includes testing half a million students in sixty-seven countries. The data from this 2015 study conclude that girls were as strong as boys in science and math in 60 percent of the PISA countries, though as individuals, girls scored even higher in reading. Boys tended to be more skilled in science and math and pursued these fields in college.

The counterintuitive information that emerged from the PISA study was this: in countries with weak legal protections for women and the least gender equality (United Arab Emirates, Algeria, Albania), the highest proportion of women chose STEM fields of study (41 percent). Conversely, in countries where women have the freest choices (Norway, Finland, Switzerland), only 20 percent were in STEM fields. In the United States the rate is 24 percent.

The PISA study can be interpreted to mean that in countries where women and men have gender equality, they may choose careers that match their strongest skills, as in liberal arts rather than in the sciences; in countries where options for women are limited and they have less social freedom, if the best career opportunities are in the sciences, then women will choose those fields.

The inescapable conclusion of the PISA study is that in free democratic societies, individuals make individual choices that are not dictated by societal gender biases.[13]

CONCLUDING WORDS AND CAVEATS FOR AMERICA'S FUTURE SURVIVAL

To advance national unity, social practices that promote accommodation and assimilation of new citizens in our country should be vigorously pursued. The opposite—the years of Balkanization promoted so damagingly by identity politics—is unhealthy for the common good. Perhaps it is too optimistic to believe that we might diminish the effects of identity politics on our country by amending our census data collection rules: in other words, maybe it is time that our federal government count us as people in the United States and stop counting us by color.

Three very different thinkers are selected for quoting here, to strengthen the ideas presented and to warn of pitfalls ahead. The late Representative Barbara Jordan of Texas was nationally distinguished as the most articulate voice in the Watergate hearings to impeach President Richard Nixon in 1972. She began life in a Black family of severe poverty and benefited from a scholarship at Mt. Holyoke College. She later was appointed by President Jimmy Carter to chair the U.S. Commission on Immigration Reform (to which I was invited to give testimony in 1990). She stated this truth: "Cultural and religious diversity does not pose a threat to the national interest as long as public policies ensure civic unity."[14]

In an op-ed by former U.S. attorney general Ed Meese and Heritage Foundation Fellow Michael Gonzalez, this statement: "Identity politics—the artificial segmentation of Americans into antagonistic groups organized along often imagined ethnic, racial and sexual categories—is tearing us apart."[15]

Father Luigi Giussani, the late Catholic monsignor of Milano, Italy, founder of the ecclesial movement, *Communion and Liberation* said this:

> The need for unity lies at the root of the whole expression of man's life; it belongs to the definition of his "I." Every great human revolution has had universalism as its supreme ideal—to make the whole of humanity one. The supreme ideal of every philosophy, too, has been the unity of mankind, a unity in which each one can be himself and yet be one with others.[16]

NOTES

1. Victor Davis Hanson, "The Origins of Our Second Civil War," *National Review*, July 31, 2018: https://www.nationalreview.com/2018/07/origins-of-second-civil-war-globalism-tech-boom-immigration-campus-radicalism/.

2. Massachusetts Public Charter Schools Association, online newsletter, April 30, 2021.

3. Paul Caron, "The Penn Law School Mob Scores a Victory," *The Wall Street Journal*, March 19, 2018.

4. Personal interview with author, 1984.

5. Amanda Kim, "Posse Boston Decision Controversy, Reignites at Posse Plus Retreat," *The Spectator*, February 16, 2020: https://spec.hamilton.edu/posse-boston-decision-controversy-reignites-at-posse-plus-retreat-99604020a647.

6. Conor Friedersdorf, "The Perils of Writing a Provocative Email at Yale," *The Atlantic*, May 26, 2016: https://www.theatlantic.com/politics/archive/2016/05/the-peril-of-writing-a-provocative-email-at-yale/484418/.

7. James Campbell, "James Baldwin's 'Cultural Appropriation—and Mine," *The Wall Street Journal*, January 29, 2021: https://www.wsj.com/articles/james-baldwins-cultural-appropriationand-mine-11611946697.

8. Campbell, "James Baldwin's 'Cultural Appropriation."

9. Campbell, "James Baldwin's 'Cultural Appropriation."

10. Thomas Chatterton Williams, "Beyond Black History Month," *The Wall Street Journal*, February 27, 2021: https://www.wsj.com/articles/beyond-black-history-month-11614355101.

11. Kyle Smith, "Happy Warrior: Segregation on the Charles," *National Review*, June 26, 2017: https://www.nationalreview.com/magazine/2017/06/26/harvard-commencement-ceremony/.

12. Smith, "Happy Warrior."

13. Susan Pinker, "Why Don't More Women Choose STEM Careers?," *The Wall Street Journal*, March 3, 2018: https://www.wsj.com/articles/why-arent-there-more-women-in-science-and-technology-1519918657.

14. Stephen Guschov, "Stopping the Drift toward Multilingualism: Why Congress Must Pass the English Language Unity Act," *Washington Times*, March 18, 2018: https://www.washingtontimes.com/news/2018/mar/7/stopping-the-drift-toward-multilingualism/.

15. Edwin Meese III and Mike Gonzalez, "Trump Can Help Overcome Identity Politics," *The Wall Street Journal*, February 28, 2018: https://www.wsj.com/articles/trump-can-help-overcome-identity-politics-1519772254.

16. *Magnificat,* vol. 20, no. 1, March 2018, 121.

4

Freedom of Speech

More Reviled than Respected in Today's USA

The First Amendment to the United States Constitution, first of the ten amendments known as the Bill of Rights, states, "Congress shall make no law respecting an establishment of religion, or prohibiting the free exercise thereof, or abridging the freedom of speech, or of the press, or the right of the people peaceably to assemble, and to petition the Government for a redress of grievances."

The rights enumerated in this amendment are powerful and clear: freedom of religion, speech, the press, assembly, and to petition the government. The assault on the right to speak, write, express opinions, or state facts has emerged as an unbridled force not only across the country, but especially in academia, the former home of open inquiry.

It would be nearly impossible to minimize the importance of this attack on one of our most fundamental rights. Not even in the heyday of wild campus activities—the vaunted 1960s—was there such widespread public action to suppress speech that does not conform to a predictable array of "progressive" positions.

Famous incidents of the past few years include the violent attacks on invited speakers at Middlebury College in Vermont, at the University of California/ Berkeley, and the University of Missouri (*Mizzou*)—all well-documented as examples of the dereliction of responsibility by college administrators. Heavy costs resulted from the attacks by masked antifa bandits at Berkeley and, in the case of the University of Missouri (Mizzou), a sharp decline in many important indices of community approval.

Since 2015, when the violence on campus gained nationwide attention, Mizzou reports that in the fall of 2017 freshmen enrollment was down by 35 percent, faculty and staff positions have been cut, dormitories shut down, and attendance at sports events significantly declined. Apparently, there are consequences for caving to student, faculty, and outside agitator violence, as much as it may be enjoyed as a popular and virtue-signaling sport by the agitators.

As a participant and a resident in an academic community for decades, observing the ways of higher education at first hand provides a clear understanding of this arena. Amherst, Massachusetts, is headquarters of the Five College Association that includes Amherst, Smith, Mt. Holyoke and Hampshire Colleges, and the University of Massachusetts.

Faculty were deeply concerned about academic freedom, fiercely determined to open up the intellectual dialogue from the stultifying narrowness of the Cold War era. The anti-war and civil rights movements of the 1960s and 1970s brought about the very changes desired, but they also began the broad redefinition of higher education.

We have five decades of well-documented accounts of the changes: fragmenting of curricula, most damagingly in the liberal arts; grade inflation; demeaning of the Western civilization that brought us to our intellectual heights; ever more focus on ethnic/racial/gender studies that evolve into victim studies and their concomitant bleating for safe spaces, claims of microaggressions and cultural misappropriation.

COLLEGE-TOWN AMHERST BEHAVES ADMIRABLY

The ramping up of attacks on free speech from coast to coast has occurred most fearsomely in the past decade. Best to begin on a positive note with a few local examples of a strong defense of free speech in these educational institutions.

Fortunately, Amherst has not experienced any violent intrusions from the thuggish antifa and their ilk. Let's look at a few instances of model behavior in our Happy Valley, home of the Five College Association. How lovely it would be to think that these acts of defense for even outrageous speech may be harbingers of a return to sanity at other school sites—one can only hope.

The useful agent for starting this conversation is Ilan Stavans, professor of Latin American Literature and Culture at Amherst College, a masterful essayist who stands out sharply from most of the *professoriat* for his balanced views. In "Teaching in the Age of Intolerance," one of his recent columns in the local newspaper, he extols the beauties of literature's classics as well as new classics being created. He speaks to the absolute need for civil exchanges of ideas among a variety of students, and deems the classroom, "the place where we fine tune our better selves."[1]

Professor Stavans, Mexican by birth, is by no means a conservative, but he is that rare human today who genuinely understands the grandeur of free expression, of listening to and learning from one another. Would that his fine qualities of attitude and character were more common in our academic precincts.

In 2013, a student group at the University of Massachusetts invited Karl Rove, political advisor to President George W. Bush in his second term, to speak on campus. On April 10 when Rove appeared, students began to disrupt his speech. The UMass chancellor, Dr. Kumble Subbaswamy, in attendance at the lecture, ordered the campus security guards to walk the loud protestors out of the auditorium, stating to the assembled that interruptions would not be tolerated. And indeed Mr. Rove's presentation went forward without further ado.

Several of the students who went to the microphone to ask a question started with this statement: "I don't agree with some of your positions, but I'm glad that you were allowed to speak." This is one instance of a university leader taking a courageous stand for freedom of speech, not in the abstract, but as a living fact in our public lives. If recent news reports are accurate, a preponderance of university and college presidents, their deans, and administrators are far too willing to bend cravenly to faculty and student pressure as in some examples that follow here.

SMITH AND MT. HOLYOKE COLLEGES: COWARDICE IN ACTION

On the negative side, locally, Smith College President Kathleen McCartney gave us two instances of rapid caving-in to mob rule. In 2014 when Cristine Lagarde, head of the International Monetary Fund (IMF), was invited to give the commencement address, student and faculty protesters were so angry and vocal that Ms. Lagarde decided to withdraw her earlier acceptance of the invitation. President McCartney made no effort on Lagarde's behalf. What an embarrassment for a single-sex women's college to demean a supremely successful leader in international banking who has nary a blemish on her *curriculum vitae*.

One year later, when the Black Lives Matter (BLM) movement appeared at Smith, this same president issued the seemingly sensible statement that "All lives matter." Oops, wrong Madame President. Immediate widespread student protests erupted and—you guessed it—she made a new announcement, retracting her words and asserting the overriding importance of BLM. February 2021 brought us a truly ugly incident at Smith that is fully described in a later essay.

Mt. Holyoke College hosted the 2018 Women of Color Trailblazers Leadership Conference, featuring guest speakers who organized the National Women's March against President Trump at his inauguration: Tamika Mallory, Carmen Perez, and Linda Sarsour. The student president of the College Republicans, Kassy Dillon, attended, excited to cover the event for her online publication, *Lone Conservative*.

However, the so-called "discussion" as the event was billed, came with strict rules: no recordings, no photographs, and no direct questions from the audience allowed. Questions must be submitted on note cards and only those preapproved would be answered by the speakers. As one may surmise, Ms. Dillon's question was not answered. But this young woman's statement at the time is simple and eloquent. While deploring the one-sided event, she said, "I welcomed the event because I believe in free speech. Instead of calling for these speakers to be disinvited, as leftist students often do, my group organized a Conservative Women Summit which featured five speakers offering different perspectives a week later . . .. I believe in civility and real discussion, so I would never disrupt an event."[2]

Not easy to find examples of courageous academics challenging the "woke" hegemony but an essay by Kalie Ward in *The Cavalier Daily*, student newspaper at the University of Virginia, does just that. She is a third-year student and a columnist for the newspaper who self-identifies as a lesbian.

Her statements reveal an intelligent nature, good practical sense, and more bravery than is shown by faculty or administrators at prestigious colleges. "Tolerance is a two-way street: U.Va. students should learn to tolerate differing beliefs," Ms. Ward's column was published in the November 2020 issue of *The Cavalier*.

A sampling of Ms. Ward's main points is evidence of her good judgment. Here are a few examples from her essay addressed to the university audience:

- when someone doesn't agree with your political or world view, they are not automatically racist. They are not automatically sexist, ableist, homophobic, transphobic, or a . . . fascist;
- I am not proud of the university culture of intolerance, of always labeling differing opinions as prejudicial;
- mindlessly shutting down our peers who don't agree with us—silencing our peers on grounds of bigotry—it is actively detracting from the university's desired culture of intellectual growth;
- the university seems to have shifted the definition of free speech to only benefit the left's political agenda.

Bravissima, Kalie Ward!

NOT A NEW PRACTICE, BUT TROUBLING NEVERTHELESS

Lest we imagine that this bending to the campus mob is a new phenomenon, it can be catalogued with an example from the 1980s featuring Linda Chavez, one-time director of the U. S. Commission on Civil Rights (1983) and editor of *American Educator* and *American Teacher*, official magazines of the American Federation of Teachers (1987). Full disclosure: Linda and I serve together on the board of directors of the Center for Equal Opportunity in Washington, DC.

Ms. Chavez was invited to deliver the commencement address at Northern Colorado University in 1989, but a few weeks before the graduation date, it was discovered that she is—*que lastima*—a conservative! Linda is what we now call Latinx and a native of Colorado by birth. Not good enough! Protests ensued and she was disinvited. In 1991 when she went to the Hostos Community College in New York to speak, she was rudely treated. These events were seemingly isolated occurrences at the time and elicited very little press coverage. They were a portent of things to come.

Before proceeding with further examples of the assaults on free speech, it is important to note that this is not merely an academic exercise, navel gazing, or the abstruse consideration of how many angels dance on the head of a pin. This assault as it has gained currency is affecting all areas of public discourse, both academic and general.

Beginning with formal speech codes introduced on college campuses, to the broad definition of "hate speech" as any idea that the listener finds uncongenial, to the "self-censorship" we all impose on ourselves and businesses impose on their advertising and employee's speech, we all accede to these impositions lest we be harshly criticized. How did we come to this in the United States? How did free speech become a coded message in the minds of those on the left for Nazism and racism?

Yet there is now an even more narrowly defined objection: that civility in public discourse is racist, an example of that other hulking monster "White privilege." It is presented to us in an article titled "Civility and White Institutional Presence: An Exploration of White Students' Understanding of Race Talk at a Traditionally White Institution," published in the *Howard Journal of Communications* at the University of Northern Idaho.

The central idea appears to be that "civility within higher education is a racialized, rather than universal norm" and that Whiteness-informed civility is something that must be stamped out. Can our popular culture become even less civil than it is, and can this be what we want to see in the halls of higher education?

To this far-left nonsense, there are finally signs of a push back. Some colleges are beginning the deliberate process of teaching students, parents, and alumni how to talk about politics and other contentious issues without going on the attack in polarized, nasty conversations. In an article describing a variety of efforts being made at Tufts, Butler, Duquesne, and Carleton, to name a few, the stated objective is to improve civil discourse.

A Knight Foundation survey of three thousand students in 2017 reports that 61 percent say the climate on their campus to stifle certain speech and the nature of social media dialogue is now less civil than a year earlier. Administrators say that the faculty need exposure to more ideological diversity if there is to be a return to policy-based debates, and to reverse the societal breakdown in civil discourse. Professor Jonathan Zimmerman at the University of Pennsylvania says it well: "The real world is full of incivility. To me that's all the more reason why our educational institutions have to try to teach a different way of being."[3]

Free speech is the element that allows us to oppose despotism in any form. Any rational person would judge attacks on free speech as the grossest from of intolerance—or so one would like to think. To judge freedom of speech for all as antithetical to equality seems a distortion of honest, moral thinking. It brings to mind a statement attributed to the English poet Samuel Taylor Coleridge in the eighteenth century: "I have seen gross intolerance shown in support of tolerance."

AMHERST'S OWN *PROVOCATEUR*: A
LEGEND IN HIS OWN TIME

For an amusing bit of relief, the politically correct town of Amherst has its very own despised "agitator." Phil O'Connell stands at the main intersection of town most days, holding a large cardboard sign with some scurrilous slogans, his favorites being attacks on feminism and "Bitch Hillary."

After the 2016 election, Mr. O'Connell appeared in front of the local high school where students were protesting the election result. His vulgar sign, "Trump has balls—you don't" earned him the contempt of all. On November 19, 2016, a young man and a young woman attacked O'Connell, knocking him to the ground and tearing up his sign. They were charged with assault and battery.

On August 24, 2017, Mr. O'Connell was physically attacked as he stood in front of the bank in the middle of town. The young man who launched the attack was arrested. Amherst Police Chief Scott Livingstone promptly announced, "We're good with protests and making sure everyone is able to legally voice their opinions . . .. The signs he's holding are not against the law and he's typically not the antagonist. Even though his political views may differ from many of those living and studying in this college town, O'Connell has First Amendment rights to free speech."[4] Thank you, Chief Livingstone, for your sensible, constitutionally correct statement.

No applause for Sarah LaCour, director of the local Business Improvement District (BID) who sent a letter to local shopkeepers on May 22, 2018, urging them not to sell any supplies to Mr. O'Connell, such as cardboard or magic markers with which he could make his signs. Now that is playing dirty pool and is definitely a form of harassment. The notion was publicly condemned and quickly dropped, but has the idea infected any of our other local merchants?

BOSTON EXCELS, THOUGH VIRTUE SIGNALING DOMINATES

George Orwell, with his prescient 1949 novel *1984*, would well understand the power of Big Brother, aka the mainstream press, in the service of the far-left wing of the Democratic Party. An example of such distortion of reality serves the point. A Boston resident, John Medlar, organized a demonstration on the Boston Common in support of free speech on August 18, 2017. The invited speaker was Professor Shiva Ayyadurai, an MIT-trained biologist and political libertarian who was brought to the United States from India as a child.

The Anti-Defamation League posted a blog about the free speech rally, to make publicly clear that the Boston rally "is not a white supremacist gathering." No matter—the event was immediately, publicly, and wrongly portrayed as a gathering of White supremacists and Nazis and counter demonstrations were organized across the state to converge on Boston.

High marks go to the Boston mayor and police for their efficient preparations to ensure a peaceful day on the Boston Common. Unlike Charlottesville where the police were ordered to "stand down" and do nothing but observe the violence, Boston rally attendees and protesters were kept apart and safe.

Forty thousand counter demonstrators assembled to express their hatred for Nazis and White Supremacists, while a very small number of free speech defenders stood their ground, totally swamped by the oh-so-virtuous and entirely misinformed crowd on a Sunday outing. Clearly people who might have attended an event in support of free speech in the public square were intimidated by the threat of violence, so often a part of left-wing protests.

The Western Massachusetts newspaper, the *Daily Hampshire Gazette*, heaped praise on the forty thousand marchers on August 20, 2017, and shamed itself in a mind-boggling editorial announcing their delight that a rally to support free speech was silenced. This truly reeks of *1984*—Doublethink and Doublespeak.

TWO GODS THAT FALTER: AAUP AND ACLU

Two organizations long esteemed as the defenders of free speech and writing on college campuses and in public life, the American Association of University Professors (AAUP) and the American Civil Liberties Union (ACLU) have both stealthily altered their policies while falsely pretending to value free speech and due process. They are no longer the champions we once admired and supported.

AMERICAN ASSOCIATION OF UNIVERSITY PROFESSORS

AAUP was once an organization that staunchly defended the rights of university professors to teach their classes and publish their scholarly papers without fear of being attacked or fired for unpopular ideas. In recent years the organization appears to be more concerned with maintaining one set of ideas—progressive—to the detriment of alternative opinions.

In a recent article, John J. Miller, director of the Dow Journalism Program at Hillsdale College, describes the new attitudes at AAUP.[5] Miller criticizes the organization for failing to make any public statement on the violent attacks at Berkeley and NYU by masked *provocateurs*. Instead, the AAUP condemns what it deems a greater threat to higher education: students who write reports on the speakers shouted down on their campuses and the pervasive far-left bias in some of their classes.

The AAUP's direct attack on student journalism is reminiscent of the professor at the University of Missouri, Melissa Click, who in 2015 called for "muscle" to remove a student reporter from documenting what was happening on the quad—and this student reporter is African American. Imagine if he had been a privileged White kid. Ms. Click was later fired from the university but the public relations disaster she helped ignite has had serious consequences, as mentioned earlier in this essay.

The AAUP has taken a leaf from the tactics of the Southern Poverty Leadership Center (SPLC), an organization that raises funds for its publishing of lists that label almost any organization that is not on the far-left as "racist." SPLC's attacks are largely inaccurate and damaging, but it is lauded by progressives, even though it was originally founded by a former KKK member, Morris Dees.

The AAUP labeled three campus organizations as promoting "witch hunts": *Campus Reform, Professor Watchlist,* and *College Fix.* As founder and director of *College Fix,* John J. Miller is adamant in speaking out on the value of his organization, which he describes as publishing "articles by student journalists, who work with our professional editors to tell true stories about campus politics and culture. Our goal is to create compelling and original content, while identifying a new generation of promising writers and editors." Good luck with that, Professor Miller.

AMERICAN CIVIL LIBERTIES UNION (ACLU)

The American Civil Liberties Union enjoyed widespread approval and support for decades for its unstinting fight for free speech and due process. Its gradual shift away from these two constitutional protections essential to a functioning democracy was not easily detected. As recently as 2017, the ACLU took a principled stand in the Charlottesville clash when a group of neo-Nazi skinheads with a permit to hold a demonstration were attacked by a larger group of counter demonstrators.

The ACLU defended the right of the original group to hold a public meeting, no matter how obnoxious their message, and criticized the Charlottesville town government for trying to cancel the permit for the event. It was an ugly scene, and it may have been the last public stance for constitutional rights by the ACLU and its traditional defense of hateful speech.

Wendy Kaminer, a former board member of the ACLU and one of its most severe critics,[6] has traced in her book the growth of partisanship at the ACLU for years. What is alarming now is the organization's turning even more sharply leftward since the 2016 election of Trump to the White House.

While faintly professing to hold to its defense of all speech, the organization declares "free speech can harm marginalized groups by undermining their civil rights. . . . Speech that denigrates such groups can inflict serious harms and is intended to and often will impede progress toward equality." These quotes are taken from "Conflicts between Competing Values or Priorities," a policy document held very closely by the ACLU but leaked nevertheless. This is a radical departure for an organization that was once famous for its singular dedication to First Amendment rights for all.

The way it will pursue its new policy guidelines is by its case selection process. As seen by its absence from recent events, the ACLU has refrained from speaking out in any cases where violence and harassment have been the actions of progressives.

The organization is on record as not opposing the heckler's veto and will not take up the defense of cases in which it does not approve the content or detects "views contrary to our values." A sad decline in their once stalwart voice, the ACLU seems to be agreeing with hard left progressives that equate words with actions, a distinction once commonly understood.[7]

PERSONAL EXAMPLES OF CANCEL CULTURE

My many experiences with speech suppression in college classrooms may be understood by describing two representative examples. The demeaning and downgrading of my work from the 1980s onward were aimed at condemning my position on the education of non-English-speaking school children. As director of a program for immigrant children in the Newton, Massachusetts, public schools, I supervised a staff of twenty-five teachers and assistants. Half a dozen of the teachers enrolled in a graduate course at Boston University that was required for job advancement.

In mid-semester they advised me that their professor warned them, in no uncertain terms, that they were not ever to use the works or ideas of Rosalie Porter in any of their term papers. Were they to cite my work in scholarly papers, they would receive a lower grade for the semester's work. My teachers were troubled by this unprofessional mandate but felt they must follow the professor's classroom instructions.

In 2002, I was co-chairman of the English for the Children campaign, a referendum question put before the voters of Massachusetts in that year's election. A student in one of the education courses at the University of Massachusetts Amherst called to inform me of this statement by her professor: "Do not bring any thoughts from Dr. Rosalie Porter into this classroom—not in our discussions or when you write your term papers."

The university where I held an undergraduate degree with high honors and an earned doctorate was so politicized that it would not invite me to speak or take part in any debate during that 2002 campaign. However, Massachusetts voters gave our referendum question 68 percent positive votes at the polls.[8]

At Marquette University in Wisconsin, a similar case occurred when Professor John McAdams was penalized for calling out a student instructor on his blog. The professor criticized graduate student instructor Cheryl Abbate "for telling an undergraduate in her ethics class that arguing against gay rights and same sex marriage was homophobic and unwelcome in her classroom." McAdams' statement was condemned by a faculty committee resulting in the president of the university agreeing to impose a punishment of two semester's unpaid leave and a demand that the professor express remorse. Shades of the old Stalinist crack downs on politically incorrect thoughts!

The university's actions led to a court case in which Professor McAdams was completely exonerated and Marquette was ordered to reinstate the professor at his same rank and pay. The case was remanded to a lower court to determine damages and back pay for him.

McAdams's attorney applauded the ruling, stating, "If academic freedom means anything, it should mean that a professor should be able to write a blog post that is accurate and of great public interest and not be disciplined for it."[9]

Incidentally, the AAUP ignored this case. It did not advocate for the academic freedom of Professor McAdams, an action that would seem totally appropriate for the organization that professes to fight for the rights of all professors.

SUMMER HI-JINKS ON MARTHA'S VINEYARD

Time to lighten up the narrative by noting a bit of summer madness that occurred on that hallowed island of all righteousness, Martha's Vineyard. In celebration of our country's founding, the great and the good of Martha's Vineyard declared Harvard University emeritus law professor Alan Dershowitz *persona non grata*. He was not to be invited to any social gatherings of these good folk or even to be given a civil greeting in public.

The man was to be shunned by all on the elite island for the 2018 season. And what is the crime that has brought this libertarian and famous defense attorney into total disrepute? Why, the man publicly stated his support for some of President Trump's policies and even met with him. Although Dershowitz is a Democrat who voted for La Hillary, his great and unforgivable sin is "aiding and abetting and *dining* with Trump."[10]

No need to weep in sympathy with the professor as he is one gutsy guy who can stand up to any mob and spew as much venom as they do. He is not sitting still for the shunning insults but is loudly and forcefully condemning his shunners. Way to go, Alan.

EARLY EXAMPLES OF COURAGE

For the optimists among us, it helps to take heart from the statements of strong-willed leaders, no matter how few there are at the moment. Claremont McKenna College saw a violent demonstration in 2017 against the invited speaker, Heather Mac Donald, Manhattan Institute Fellow and author of *The War on Cops*. Student protestors blockaded the entrance to the auditorium and spent the evening chanting "No cops, no KKK, no fascist USA." The speaker ended up addressing an almost empty hall.

In a statement, the college declared, "The blockade breached institutional values of freedom of expression and assembly. Furthermore, this action violated policies of both the College and the Claremont Colleges that prohibit material disruption of college programs and create unsafe conditions in disregard of state law." The punishment for the ten students who violated college rules was suspension, signaling that Claremont is keeping its promise to protect free speech on campus.

President Chodosh wrote a fine statement following the protest: "The breach of our freedoms to listen to views that challenge us and to engage in dialogue about matters of controversy is a serious, ongoing concern we must address effectively."[11]

At the University of California, Berkeley, the campus that became famous for the free speech movement in the wild and wooly 1960s, violent protests during the 2016–2017 academic year finally tested the patience of university leaders. Not only did violence by students and antifa masked agitators erupt against speakers (Milo Yannoupulos, Ann Coulter) but their actions cost the university $2 million to repair damages to campus property and provide security. The tolerance for these shenanigans has evaporated.

Chancellor Carol Christ declared 2017 "Free Speech Year" in a statement to the campus community: "The University has the responsibility to provide safety and security for its community and guests, and we will invest the necessary resources to achieve that goal. If you choose to protest, do so peacefully. That is your right and we will defend it with vigor. We will not tolerate violence, and we will hold anyone accountable who engages in it."[12]

Erwin Chemerinsky, newly installed dean of the Law School at Berkeley in 2017, added his voice in support of universal freedom of speech. He reminds us that in the heyday of the 1960s movement actions, students were demonstrating in favor of free speech at Berkeley; today they argue against it. They want to protect their classmates from hate speech.

Dean Chemerinsky cites a Pew Research study reporting that 4 in 10 students today believe they should be able to forcibly stop people from making statements that are offensive to minority groups. The dean's arrival at Berkeley is providential. He "gets it."[13]

These laudable signs from a few stalwart leaders in academia are merely a miniscule turn around in the poisonous new religion of intolerance, but they are something. Where will these student activists go with their virtuous, violence-approving ideas after their college studies end?

How truly appalling it is that positions in support of free speech are now considered unusual, even courageous, an unmistakable sign of just how dire things are on campus today. Political and cultural views inevitably are destined to change. There are very narrow legal justifications for the suppression of speech in extreme situations, but they do not include shouting down or assaulting invited speakers.

Can any truly democratic republic tolerate violent actions to "cleanse" our public life from any word, speaker, or idea that may not pass sensitivity muster? This would seem a good topic for debate with incoming freshmen each year.

NOTES

1. Ilan Stavans, "'Friday Takeaway': Teaching in the Age of Intolerance," *Daily Hampshire Gazette*, June 16, 2017: https://www.gazettenet.com/First-Person -10660157.

2. Kassy Dillon, "The Women's March Holds a One-Way 'Discussion,'" *The Wall Street Journal*, April 12, 2018: https://www.wsj.com/articles/the-womens-march -holds-a-one-way-discussion-1523574525.

3. Melissa Korn, "With Civil Discourse 101, Colleges Address Campus Climate," *The Wall Street Journal*, August 17, 2018.

4. *Daily Hampshire Gazette*, September 5, 2017.

5. John J. Miller, "Who's Afraid of Student Journalists?" *The Wall Street Journal*, February 9, 2017: https://www.wsj.com/articles/whos-afraid-of-student-journalists -1486597340.

6. Wendy Kaminer, *Worst Instincts: Cowardice, Conformity and the ACLU* (Boston: Beacon Press, 2009).

7. Wendy Kaminer, "The ACLU Retreats from Free Expression," *The Wall Street Journal*, June 21, 2018, and Wendy Kaminer and Alan Dershowitz, "Where's the ACLU When You Need It?," *The Wall Street Journal*, May 11, 2017.

8. Rosalie Pedalino Porter, *American Immigrant: My Life in Three Languages* (Piscataway, NJ: Transaction Publishers, 2011).

9. Melissa Korn, "Professor Wins College-Freedom Case in Wisconsin," *The Wall Street Journal*, July 7, 2018.

10. Mark Shanahan, "The Vineyard Gives Dershowitz a Cold Shoulder," *The Boston Globe*, July 4, 2018.

11. Sophie Mann, "Claremont's Social Justice Warriors Face the Music," *National Review*, July 31, 2017.

12. John Montanari, "Cites Carol Christ's Defense of Free Speech," *Daily Hampshire Gazette*, September 6, 2017.

13. Erwin Chemerinsky, "Hate Speech Is Protected Speech Even on College Campuses," *Vox*, December 26, 2017: https://www.vox.com/the-big-idea/2017/10/25 /16524832/campus-free-speech-firstamendment-protest.

5

Freedom of Religious Practice

The practice of religion in America and the Western world has undergone some possibly cataclysmic upheavals in the last half century. Since the turbulent 1960s, the numbers of religious practitioners in the Christian developed world have dropped dramatically. In America, in the past two decades, Christian religious observers have been reduced from 77 percent to 65 percent.

Secularization of modern society, the culture conflicts almost completely won by the progressive left and laws inhibiting Christian symbols in public life, have taken their toll. For the Roman Catholic Church, the public revelations of priests' sexual abuse of young people have had a profound effect on the number of Catholics who remain loyal and continue church attendance.

The women's liberation movement began, from the early 1970s, to exert its influence as one of the strongest players in forcing cultural change, demoting the importance of the traditional two-parent family and parents' roles in child rearing. Scorn for the importance of marriage and the two-parent family is just one example of the forces that encouraged the disappearance of religious norms.

Dwelling on the obstructions to religious health in modern society, there are welcome new sources of sound ideas from all sides of the ideological spectrum. A publication from 2016 provides a well-rounded review of religious trends in the United States for the past seventy-five years, *Getting Religion: Faith, Culture and Politics from the Age of Eisenhower to the Era of Obama*. The author, Kenneth Woodward, was religion editor for *Newsweek* magazine for thirty-eight years. The title is slightly misleading as the book is not about "becoming" religious; it is a well-written account of the various flavors of religious activity that held sway in this country from the 1950s to the present day.

It is familiar territory for mature adults, cavorting through these popular fancies. Woodward does a masterful job of presenting the popular trends: rejection of 1950s "square" traditionalism, 1960s hippie-dom, and liberation

45

theology supporting populist movements in Central America and Cuba. Then, he delves into the love of Buddha and takes us through the heyday of Protestant evangelicalism, with such leaders as Billy Graham, and the deep fissures in Protestant congregations over women priests, sexual identity, and more. He makes it all so accessible, lucid, and timely.

The attacks on religious liberty and free expression across the West in recent decades is troubling and is not focused on Judeo-Christian communities alone. An essay by the Dalai Lama suggests that religion faces three main challenges: communism, science, and consumerism. His statements are simply couched yet eloquent:

> Today the world faces a crisis related to lack of respect for spiritual principles and ethical values. . . . Self-discipline and self-restraint of all citizens—from CEOs to lawmakers to teachers—are needed to create a good society. But these virtues . . . require inner cultivation. This is why spirituality and religion are relevant in the modern world. . . . I promote this type of secularism: to be a kind person who does not harm others regardless of profound religious differences.
>
> Communism controls religious institutions and the education system in Tibet, teaching children that Buddhism is old-fashioned. . . . Modern science up until now has confined itself to studying only phenomena that are material in nature . . . neglecting the study of Buddhist principles such as rebirth. . . . Religion values ethical conduct, which may involve delayed gratification, whereas consumerism directs us toward immediate happiness . . . that happiness comes from external objects.[1]

This Buddhist leader, the 145th Dalai Lama, ends his essay on a hopeful note, encouraging us to "study the Buddha's teachings, you may find some of them are in harmony with your view of societal values, science and consumerism—and some of them are not. That is fine. Continue to investigate and reflect on what you discover."

Fine words, but it is hard to imagine they might lead to positive outcomes. We cannot evade the fact that Tibet has been controlled by China for almost a century with little or no sign of its ever achieving its own sovereignty and free practice of its Buddhist religion.[2]

EFFECTS OF IMMIGRATION FROM THE MIDDLE EAST

The assaults on Christianity in Western Europe and the United States contain some similarities and a few very real differences. The supra-national experiment that created the European Union in the 1990s expanded membership from the United Kingdom to Greece and the former Communist bloc countries of Eastern Europe.

The EU has brought solidarity and economic improvements to countries largely rebuilt after World War II. Common governance from Brussels, a human rights court of appeals in The Hague, a common currency and free passage of EU citizens among all these nations are documented positives.

The EU countries in recent decades have experienced a decline in the practice of religion—a strong turn to secularism—and a dramatic drop in birth rates. In Italy and Ireland, for example, the birth rate is below the replacement level.

Calamitous internecine struggles in Middle Eastern and African countries have brought ever larger numbers of migrants and refugees to Europe seeking asylum and economic opportunity. Since 2018, Germany's unilateral policy of inviting 1.2 million refugees to enter Europe is proving to have devastating effects. Almost entirely Muslim entrants, less than half are refugees from war-torn Syria, for whom the policy was originally announced—the rest are young men seeking work, not refugees in the classic sense but economic migrants.

Muslim communities in all Western European countries have been expanding for the past few decades and demonstrate a solid cohesiveness, very little evidence of adapting to the culture of democracies and secular society. European leaders and elites struggle heroically to welcome new immigrants, to accommodate and support their needs, but it is a very strained fit.

Between the Europeans who believe in such basics as division of church and state, equal education for women, individual rights of speech and association, and the practitioners of Islam for whom these ideas are anathema, there exists an almost unbridgeable chasm, especially for those Muslims who subscribe to Sharia law.

The "clash of civilizations" we see playing out today was anticipated a quarter century ago by Harvard professor Samuel Huntington in his prescient essay of that title. His book, *The Clash of Civilizations and the Remaking of World Order* (1996) stirred up the political science world greatly. Huntington's major forecast for the post–Cold War period after 1990 is that the primary axis of conflict will be along cultural lines, not between nations.

It is beyond the scope of this narrative to provide an extended review of all the attacks on free speech and accepted behavior of young women in EU countries by Islamic fundamentalists. From the murders of Charlie Hebdo writers, assassinations in Holland and life threats against legislators, sexual attacks on young women at social events, and the horrific terrorist mass killings in France, England, Belgium, and Scandinavia—the litany is long, with each new outrage receiving full press coverage. Here are a few quotes from an article by Ross Douthat, columnist for the *New York Times*:

[I]t is hard enough for a political union to reconcile the different branches of the West—German and Mediterranean, French and Anglo-Saxon. It becomes harder when that same union is trying to manage a society so multicultural—as European nations under the pressure of mass migration may become—as to lack religious or linguistic or historical common ground.[3]

Today's Western nationalists argue, plausibly, that many European distinctives are unlikely to survive if nation-states are weak, mass immigration constant, Christianity and Judaism replaced by indifferentism and Islam, and young elites educated as global citizens without knowing their own home—not when religious practice is so weak, patriotism so attenuated, the continent's birth rate so staggeringly low.[4]

COLLISION OF RELIGIOUS FREEDOM
AND SPECIAL GROUP RIGHTS

In taking up the subject of attitudes toward religious practices in our country, there is a broad, ongoing debate dealing with the philosophical, historical, and policy dimensions of religious liberty, why it matters, and how it ought to be protected. On the emotionally fraught issues across the country regarding certain laws, an excellent resource for the debate is provided in the book by John Corvino, Ryan T. Anderson, and Sherif Girgis, *Debating Religious Liberty and Discrimination* (2017).

The basic differences among civil libertarians may be seen as the concerns on one side of the argument, that is, that religious conservatives are trying to attack and harm the identity and dignity of the LGBTQ community; while on the opposite side, religious conservatives see that their deeply held beliefs are being marginalized and scorned.

A healthy discussion of what discrimination is, when it is unjust and when it ought to be unlawful, is one of the best features of this book. Corvino cites the Hobby Lobby case decided by the U.S. Supreme Court in 2014 as a chief example for the negative effects of allowing a religious exemption for a Christian-owned corporation. He argues against religious exemptions from generally applicable laws because these exemptions can cause harm to minorities—people who are already at a disadvantage, socially and economically.

The Hobby Lobby ruling, in fact, justified the right of the company to hold to its Christian principles, which forbade paying for certain procedures. In *Burwell v. Hobby Lobby*, the U.S. Supreme Court ruled "that the contraceptive mandate under the Patient Protection and Affordable Care Act violated a privately held, for-profit corporation's right to religious freedom."[5]

Hobby Lobby pays for its employee's health insurance coverage, including a number of different forms of contraception. The company is fulfilling its obligations to employees within its religious convictions. They do not pay for abortion-inducing medications or gender-altering surgery. Corvino's main argument against the Hobby Lobby ruling rests on his notion that people are not treated equally in the implementation of anti-discrimination laws, a moral shortcoming.

In the view on the other side of this debate, the LGBTQ complaint of discrimination does not meet the threshold that would merit government intervention restricting religious freedom. Anderson and Girgis present their observations on discrimination, which may be more persuasive. These two scholars argue that, in general, it is a matter of how people make moral judgments and that reasonable people can consider certain cases on their merits—all instances of discrimination are not the same.

We may say that a Catholic hospital's refusal to perform sex reassignment surgery may be legitimate, but it would not be acceptable for that hospital to refuse to provide a cancer treatment to a transgender patient. For a florist to refuse to arrange flowers for a same-sex wedding on religious grounds may pass muster, while that same florist will sell flowers of any sort to a gay customer—the situations are clearly different. These distinctions are not accepted by Corvino, who apparently wants no religious scruples to hold sway, ever.

Some will agree with Anderson and Girgis that the new wave of laws purporting to protect sexual orientation and gender identity amount to a threat to religious freedom. These two legal scholars do strongly argue this position, while their coauthor Corvino is just as committed to the opposite view. Altogether, the three authors are to be admired for addressing this subject, and for their ability to disagree in a civil manner, engaging with one another thoughtfully—talents not too much in evidence in contemporary America.

A recent case in this genre illustrates the reluctance of the Supreme Court justices to take any bold steps. It is the *Masterpiece Cakeshop v. Colorado Civil Rights Commission* decision in 2018. The baker refused to design a special wedding cake for a same-sex couple. In a 7–2 decision (Justices Ginsburg and Sotomayor dissenting), the court sided with the baker, asserting that the Colorado Civil Rights Commission violated the free exercise of religion rights of the baker. However, the Supreme Court has yet to rule on the broad principal issue—the intersection of anti-discrimination laws, free exercise of religion, and freedom of speech.

THE POLITICALLY TOXIC SUBJECT OF
ABORTION: A TANGENTIAL ISSUE

Since the 1973 United States Supreme Court decision in *Roe v. Wade* declared abortion to be a new constitutional right, the issue has received consistent and fiery public discussion from supporters and opponents. Let it be stated from the outset: the original argument for passing *Roe v. Wade* as a new right in the U.S. Constitution is understood by legal experts on both liberal and conservative sides to have been entirely faulty.

The Supreme Court does not have the power to change the Constitution, while states are fully empowered to pass laws on abortion. There are two ways to amend the U.S. Constitution:

- The Constitution may be amended by a two-thirds vote of Congress.
- The Constitution may be amended by a Convention voted on by Congress in response to applications from two-thirds of state legislatures.

Unfortunately, the battle lines were drawn early, and each side appears to hold to the most extreme and rigid positions. On one side, abortion is an essential part of a woman's health care. Medication, surgery, or procedures must ensure her right to choose when and how to end an unwanted pregnancy. This position is guaranteed in the *Roe v. Wade*, ruling which does not provide details but is a federal umbrella.

The strongest rebuttal to this view is the "right to life" movement, opposing all abortion rights from a religious conviction that human life begins at conception, that it is at all times "virtual infanticide." Christians, most fervently Catholics, hold this view.

Fifty years of public actions to promote one side or the other through legal challenges, street protests, restrictive state laws, and harassment at abortion clinics have hardened into political positions. Although the Democratic party traditionally counts most Catholics among its voters, the party consistently supports unfettered abortion rights. The Republican party is a bit more nuanced in its stance. Many in the party are not opposed to abortion, they tend more to align with states' rights advocacy for some restrictions.

Without dwelling on the fifty years of history of the abortion skirmishes, it is fair to state that at this moment in 2022 both sides are at a pivotal point in the coming months. Progressives have won victories in several states in recent years expanding abortion rights, while abortion opponents have gained restrictions in other states.

New York's Reproductive Health Act, passed by the legislature and signed by Governor Andrew Cuomo in January 2019, conveys abortion rights further into the term of pregnancy and lowers the age for women to have the procedure without parental approval. Nurse practitioners and mid-wives may perform abortions and no connection to a hospital in case of emergencies is required. Perhaps the most significant new expansive right in this act is that a patient may decide that there is a physical or mental health risk—at any time during the pregnancy. It appears to sanction the procedure up to the last day of pregnancy.

At the time, Governor Cuomo was not shy about his support for this law, with a celebratory event at the State House in Albany. This event was accompanied by the governor's order that the World Trade Center and other New York landmarks be illuminated with pink lights to further publicize the signing of the Reproductive Health Act. It doesn't get much gaudier or more boastful than that.[6]

RESTRICTIONS AT THE STATE LEVEL

Abortion opponents have succeeded in passing state laws restricting the procedure in various ways, mainly by extending the number of weeks that abortion is banned. One of the cases that is typical of the restrictions now awaiting higher ruling is Missouri's HB 126, which bans abortion after eight weeks.

The law was passed by the Missouri legislature and signed by Governor Mike Parsons in August 2019. However, the day before it was to go to into effect, the Eighth Circuit Court placed an injunction on most parts of the bill, effectively stopping its enforcement.[7]

The most extreme restriction appears in Texas Senate Bill 8, the Heartbeat Act, that went into effect on September 1, 2021. It forbids abortion after evidence of a fetal heartbeat or at about six weeks. It has an unusual new feature: it allows private citizens to sue any doctor who performs an abortion after the presence of a fetal heartbeat, considering that action a violation of the law.[8]

The principal player in abortion politics was named in May 2021 when the Supreme Court announced it will hear a Mississippi case: *Dobbs v. Jackson Women's Health Organization*. This is the case that will test the mettle of the justices. There are two separate elements to the Mississippi case: (1) it asks whether a state can ban abortion before viability (usually twenty-four to twenty-six weeks of pregnancy); and (2) the blockbuster appeal—it is asking the Supreme Court to overturn *Roe v. Wade* outright.[9]

CATHOLIC POLITICIANS AND
JUDGES AND ABORTION

How will the justices approach the Mississippi case and the other related abortion cases they are scheduled to hear in the 2021–2022 session? The last time the U.S. Supreme Court favored *Roe v. Wade* as an "essential holding" was in the 1992 *Planned Parenthood v. Casey* ruling. The 2021 court now seats a 6–3 majority who lean conservative, though Chief Justice Roberts often joins the more liberal wing. A fact also being noted is that five of the justices are known to be practicing Catholics (Alito, Barrett, Thomas, Roberts, and Cavanaugh).

It is here that the issue of political expediency and religious beliefs clash and facile assumptions must be reexamined. While the subject is too broad for this essay, raising the question with a few illustrative examples may encourage readers to pay attention to the court issue and to the coming actions that will be taken by politicians and judges.

Do all Catholic politicians oppose abortion rights and have they so acted on this issue in their legislative efforts? The answer is one of timing. During his presidency, Bill Clinton pronounced a moderate view, often quoted since 1992, that abortion should be "safe, legal, and rare." That sentiment is unmentionable in 2022 as the Democratic Party has swerved very far left on this issue.

The most prominent politicians to observe today are House Speaker Nancy Pelosi and President Biden, both Roman Catholics. Their public statements show their unwavering support for abortion rights, with no restrictions, and the necessity of fighting any challenges to overturn *Roe v. Wade*.

This coming season of the Supreme Court may reveal how strongly the Catholic justices hew to their promises that their personal beliefs are not the basis of legal decisions. Already the court has brought strong condemnation on itself for not banning the Texas Heartbeat Law immediately but allowing it to go into effect for the time being.

President Biden is the prime player as it is reported that he instructed Attorney General Merrick Garland to sue the State of Texas over its fetal heartbeat law within days of its passage.[10] Biden practices his Catholic religion publicly, but he appears to have no qualms about fighting the abortion battles firmly on the side of unlimited abortion rights.

House Speaker Pelosi follows the same private/public pattern. On September 3, 2021, she announced that a bill would be introduced in the House of Representatives later in the month, "The Women's Health Protection Act." The speaker is not moderate or neutral in her comments on the Supreme Court's refusal to ban the Texas law immediately: "The Supreme

Court's cowardly, dark-of-night decision to uphold a flagrantly unconstitutional assault on women's rights and health is staggering . . . necessitating codifying *Roe v. Wade*."[11]

One of the most extreme models for an elected politician of moral conscience comes to mind. Father Robert Drinan, a Jesuit priest, was elected to the U.S. Congress to represent the City of Newton, a wealthy, socially progressive community of a hundred thousand residents in the Boston area. An interesting aspect of Newton's election of Drinan to the House of Representatives in 1970 is the fact that 40 percent of Newton's voters are Jewish.

Drinan was reelected four times, serving from 1971 to 1981, and was much admired for his liberal, progressive views. He vehemently opposed the Vietnam War and called for Republican President Richard Nixon to be impeached. For a Catholic priest and a Jesuit, his stated position was that while he was personally opposed to abortion, considering it "virtual infanticide," its legality was a separate issue from its morality—a model for an elected official who would not allow his morals to interfere with his political conscience.

In 1980 Father Drinan's career as a legislator was ended by order of his religious superior, not by the voters of Newton, Massachusetts. Pope John Paul II demanded that all priests withdraw from electoral politics. Father Drinan obeyed and thus ended his career in politics. His statement on that event was this: "It is unthinkable . . . .. I am proud and honored to be a priest and a Jesuit. As a person of faith, I must believe that there is work for me to do which will somehow be more important than the work I am required to leave."[12]

The Supreme Court heard arguments on December 1, 2021, in the *Mississippi Gestational Age Act, HB 1510*. Adam Liptak wrote in the *New York Times*, "The Supreme Court heard arguments in a case that concerns a Mississippi law which bans abortions after15 weeks of pregnancy and challenges the 1973 *Roe v. Wade* decision . . . . On average, it takes the court about three months after an argument to issue a decision."[13]

How the U.S. Supreme Court decides the abortion conundrum this term, whether to take a major step in reviving the *Roe v. Wade* constitutional question or to issue a very narrow ruling and evade the larger question, remains to be seen.

WHAT MIGHT HAVE BEEN

A moderate route might have been agreed on years ago by the voters, elected officials, and judges in our states—not "all or nothing" but reasonable limits on a procedure that deserves legitimacy in a nation such as the United

States with the highest level of diversity of any developed nation. Not totally outlawing abortion to satisfy people with moral compunctions, but allowing the procedure with reasonable restrictions to respect the nation's varieties of religious beliefs. That has not been the case.

An international perspective on abortion rights is useful in comparing what limits are allowed. Marc A. Thiessen, in the *Washington Post* on December 2, 2021, reports that the United States is one of just seven out of 198 countries that allows elective abortions after twenty weeks of pregnancy:

> [T]wo of the others are China and North Korea. By contrast, 39 of 42 European nations—including France and Germany—bar elective abortions at 15 weeks of less. . . . Not one permits them through all nine months of pregnancy as do seven states and the District of Columbia.[14]

CHRISTIAN SYMBOLS AND OBSERVANCES DISAPPEAR FROM A TOWN: PERSONAL TESTAMENT

An account of five decades in a New England college town will round out this treatise on religion as its symbols have been displayed, then diminished, and "disappeared"—an evolution. On arriving in Amherst, Massachusetts, in the 1960s, every facet of life in academia and the ways of a small, "town and gown" community were appealing.

Christmas brought our young family to the Town Common where, on a clear, chilly evening there was the ceremonial lighting of the Merry Maple Christmas Tree, group singing of traditional carols, and a welcome serving of hot chocolate for all. Prominently on display on the Town Common was a large crèche representing the figures of the Nativity, which remained until the end of the twelve days of Christmas.

On a hill beside the entrance to Amherst College, the most majestic fir tree was decorated with colored lights. The Amherst public library featured a large pine tree decorated with lights in the children's reading room.

On Easter Saturday, a large banner over the main street of town with the title "Christ is Risen" announced the public ceremony at dawn on Easter Sunday morning on the Town Common, welcoming all.

Over the next three decades, it all gradually disappeared. No longer is a crèche displayed (the excuse being that vandals were damaging the figures); the lighting of the "Merry Maple" continued, but the singing of carols evolved to more commercial ballads; the observance was not only about Christmas but inclusive of Channukah and Kwanzaa, a newly minted observance imported from Africa; no lights on the Amherst College hill or on the façade of the Students' Union—a student had objected that any Christian symbol was offensive to him.

Amherst schools eliminated the traditional student performances of Christmas plays or songs. The national holiday began to be officially designated not "Christmas vacation" but "Winter vacation." Being a rebel, I asked permission at the town library to bring cookies and read a few holiday books to the young children, which I was allowed to do, even though my home-baked cookies were Christmas-tree shaped.

Soon there was a new religious symbol in the middle of town—for the eight days of Channukah there is a giant electric Menorah installed on the Town Common. Each evening, one electric candle is lit. No one objects, of course, and no one should. In the spring, for the Jewish festival of Succot, there is a symbolic straw hut on the common.

Many strong objections against the sign for the Easter Sunday Service began to be heard. The "Christ is Risen" banner flying over the middle of town for a few days before Easter was now deemed offensive. Some objected that such a sign made the town look like a place for religious fanatics. The ceremony, once an annual tradition of the South Amherst Congregational Church, was canceled. Amherst, Massachusetts, has been thoroughly purified of Christian symbols in the public square.

WHAT ARE OUR PUBLICLY APPROVED RELIGIOUS IDEALS IN THIS MILLENNIUM?

Traditional religions have been stigmatized by the new fundamentalism and culturally ascendant secularism. The new dominant belief systems are dogmatic, "substitute" faiths: climate change extremism, and the "new anti-racism." The patron saint in the climate change religion can only be the young Scandinavian maiden Greta Thunberg, representing the Biblical admonition "and the children shall lead them." The new anti-racism idols are many, with Ibram X. Kendi, Ta-Nahesi Coates, Isabel Wilkerson, and Robin DiAngelo holding pride of place.

The old religions believed in and promoted positive concepts: redemption for sinful behavior, humanitarian values of charity and love, and achieving contemplative inner peace. The new belief systems instead are basically wedded to manipulative hysteria, fear, and anger to a future of doom.

True believers must not deviate publicly from the prescriptive truths of "systemic/structural racism" or any scientific evidence challenging the party line on global warming. The punishments are "cancel culture" for such heresies. Being "canceled" may involve any punishment from public shaming to loss of reputation or loss of employment.

And this swift destruction of personal reputations does not stop with one's death. Serious "culture warriors" seem bent on searching world history to winnow out some flagrant word spoken or act committed long, long ago. Leafing through a new issue of the scholarly magazine *Academic Questions*, I caught a glimpse in passing of the outing of our late silent movie star Lillian Gish for the sin of appearing in the movie *The Birth of a Nation* in 1915. Trashing her reputation long after she has left this earth seems mean spirited, but we are supposed to judge everything by our higher sensitivity and brain power of today.

Professional football player Tim Tebow was universally condemned for daring to kneel for a brief prayer before games. Yet Colin Kaepernick is a national hero since 2016 for starting the public fad of athletes kneeling during the national anthem to protest racial inequality and police brutality. This is a mysterious practice for African American athletes who are the most highly paid workers in the economy of this hated United States.

In the 2021 Olympic trials in Japan, U.S. hammer throw star Gwen Berry displayed her disdain for America. At the ceremony to celebrate her success, she deliberately turned away from the singing of the national anthem of the country that has given her the training and opportunity to excel in her sport. It leads one to believe that anti-racism trumps sports and national pride in sports achievements.

Tidying up the loose ends of the wayward explorations in the arena of religion and religious observances in their various guises circa 2022, it would be best to end with some mildly ambiguous quotes to ponder. Surely a bit of dry humor cannot go amiss. The preference is up to the reader.

"If a thing is worth doing, it is worth doing badly."

—G. K. Chesterton, English sage

"Anything worth doing, is worth to doing to excess."

—Nantucket Island *bon vivant,* Alby Silva

NOTES

1. Dalai Llama, "How to Be a Buddhist in Today's World," *The Wall Street Journal,* July 6, 2017: https://www.wsj.com/articles/how-to-be-a-buddhist-in-todays-world -1499381040?mod=e2two.

2. Dalai Llama, "How to Be a Buddhist in Today's World."

3. Ross Douthat, "The West and What Comes After," *The New York Times*, July 8, 2017: https://www.nytimes.com/2017/07/08/opinion/sunday/the-west-and-what -comes-after.html.

4. Douthat, "The West and What Comes After."

5. Wikipedia, *Burwell v. Hobby Lobby Stores, Inc.*, September 23, 2021: https://en .wikipedia.org/wiki/Burwell_v._Hobby_Lobby_Stores,_Inc.

6. Joseph Spector and Jon Campbell, "Abortion Laws in NY: How They Changed with the Reproductive Health Act," *Democrat & Chronicle*, January 22, 2019: https: //www.democratandchronicle.com/story/news/politics/albany/2019/01/22/abortion -laws-new-york-how-they-change-immediately/2643065002/.

7. Kaitlyn Schallhorn, "Missouri Abortion Ban Blocked, but Some HB 126 Provisions Implemented," *The Missouri Times*, August 28, 2019.

8. Erin Douglas, "Texas Abortion Law a 'Radical Expansion' of Who Can Sue Whom, and an About-face for Republicans on Civil Lawsuits," *The Texas Tribune*, September 3, 2021.

9. Elizabeth Nash et al., "Mississippi Is Attacking *Roe v. Wade* Head On— the Consequences Could Be Severe," *Guttmacher Institute*, August 17, 2021: https://www.guttmacher.org/article/2021/08/mississippi-attacking-roe-v-wade-head -consequences-could-be-severe.

10. Sadie Gurman and Brent Kendall, "Biden Administration Sues Texas Over Its Abortion Law," *The Wall Street Journal*, September 10, 2021: https://www.wsj.com /articles/biden-administration-expected-to-file-suit-soon-challenging-texas-abortion -law-11631205764.

11. Jacob Gershman, "Justices' Abortion Decision Sets Off Scramble," *The Wall Street Journal*, September 3, 2021.

12. Mark Feeney, "Congressman-Priest Drinan Dies," *The Boston Globe*, January 29, 2007.

13. Adam Liptak. "The Supreme Court Seems Poised to Uphold Mississippi's Abortion Law." *New York Times*, December 1, 2021: https://www.nytimes.com/live /2021/12/01/us/abortion-mississippi-supreme-court.

14. Marc A. Thiessen, "On Abortion, the Supreme Court Is Set to Overturn Decades of Wrongs," *Washington Post*, December 2, 2021: https://www.washingtonpost.com/ opinions/2021/12/02/abortion-supreme-court-kavanaugh-plessy-mississippi/.

6

Race and the New "Anti-Racism"

Developments Post George Floyd, 2020–2022

The professional experiences and observations documented in this narrative, beginning in 2018, are suddenly overwhelmed, starting in 2020, by the sudden crushing impact of the coronavirus pandemic, and the new "anti-racism" agenda gone ballistic.

It is reasonable to say that our country was not prepared for the fierceness, the hatefulness, and the all-consuming power of the Black Lives Matter movement that emerged newly strengthened after the death of George Floyd. An instantaneous shift occurred from our concerns over the global pandemic starting in March 2020, to the immediate eruption of powerful protests, violence, rioting, burning, and looting that surged in several cities in the summer months of that year.

Events of this magnitude have certainly happened before in past decades, most notably the riots in Newark, Washington, and New York City after the assassination of Martin Luther King, Jr.; the 1968 riots in Chicago at the Democratic Party Convention; and on other occasions over police abuses of unarmed men.

The ferocity of the actions taken in major cities spread immediately, especially in Minneapolis, Seattle, and Portland, to name the most damaged. In Portland, Oregon, for example, violence totaled over five months of nightly outrage. How do we account for the exaggerated, prolonged actions, and can we posit the possible main causes? It should not be necessary to state the obvious—that peaceful protest is a basic right in our democratic society—but it must be restated here to avoid any misunderstanding. My own participation in a variety of antiwar, pro–civil rights, peaceful protests of the past is amply noted in my writings.

Opinions vary. One clear reason may be the age and communications combo: young people had been in lockdown since March 2020 due to the pandemic, unable to study much, travel, or work outside their living places, and they had lots of pent-up energy. Consider this cohort with its heavy engagement on social media and the George Floyd scene and you have the perfect storm—a righteous combustion of mob behavior.

Black Lives Matter and antifa played a large part in inspiring and supplying support for violent attacks on public monuments and buildings, and the establishment of a section of Seattle as a private zone from which to attack police. Unlawful acts in that Seattle zone resulted in a few rapes and deaths, while police and ambulance entry to rescue victims was barred.

How does this behavior, which was observed daily on television news programs, lead to a redressing of racial wrongs? What does "end racism" mean as a viable objective? Is this vague goal, nowhere buttressed with details except the constant cry to condemn all "Whites" and our entire country, the only game in town?

GOVERNMENT RESPONSES TO VIOLENT DEMONSTRATIONS

The most crucial element that accounts for the obscene extent of the violence is the response of local and state officials who tacitly and openly failed to condemn the violence and even joined in some of the protests (mayors of Portland, Seattle, and New York City). That the federal police were finally sent to Portland is a testament to the level of uncontrolled criminal activity, after fifty-five days of violence in the city streets, and the repeated attempts to burn down a federal court house and a police station.

The irony of the courthouse chosen for destruction is that it is named for a Japanese American hero of World War II, Pvt. Nakamura, not for some Confederate general. Black Lives Matter–supported riots appeared to make no distinction among sites to be leveled. We should not miss the irony that Portland vehemently resisted help from federal police, maintaining that they could protect their own city—an enormous lie.

THE WASHINGTON, DC, CAPER: JANUARY 6, 2021

In January and February 2021, the capitol of our country could not get enough National Guard troops stationed in the city to protect our legislators. Surely after the Congressional buildings had been secured with fencing and barbed wire, weeks after the outrageous attack on the U.S. Congress of January 6, the National Guard troops should have been sent home. But Speaker Pelosi was adamant that they must remain—six thousand strong—until the end of March 2021, or until fall, or forever. The National Guard troops were finally sent home by the end of the summer.

The January 6, 2021, raid of the halls of Congress in our national capital was a terrible event, of course. No justification can ever be made for the riotous actions. It was a demonstration that got greatly out of hand. Barriers have been installed to prevent such an intrusion from ever being repeated. Some queries were raised publicly as to why the warnings to the FBI and DC police before the riots were not heeded with increased security since National Guard troops were nearby. That topic seemed to disappear quickly from the media's attention.

The rounding up and arresting of hundreds of rioters was carried out assiduously. The fact that over one hundred are still in custody awaiting trial gives one a moment for pause—why is this taking so long? Were all the culprits White supremacists or were some people swept up by mistake?

However, now that the country has had a year to investigate the January 6 riot and a Congressional Committee empaneled for the purpose, there is some disputation beginning to emerge. Roger Kimball is the author of several books on American culture, including *The Long March: How the Revolution of the 1960s Changed America* (2000). On September 20, 2021, he gave a lecture on the subject of January 6 at a Hillsdale College symposium. The title of his talk was "The January 6 Insurrection Hoax."

Kimball's research leads to a presentation of facts at odds with many of the accepted "truths" so continually repeated by the Democratic Party and the mainstream press. The facts, well-documented by Kimball, are summarized here, beginning with the exact words of former President Trump who did not incite the overthrow of the government but actually told demonstrators to march to the Capitol peacefully and patriotically.

Compared to the riots over several months of the summer of 2020 that caused over a billion dollars in property damages and the deaths of twenty people, the DC event lasted only a few hours with damages estimated to be about $1.5 million according to U.S. prosecutors. Only one person was killed, an unarmed woman protester, Ashli Babbitt, who was shot by a Capitol Police officer. We've learned only recently that some who planned to intrude in the halls of Congress deliberately stowed their guns away from the scene. And while most participants did not seem to be carrying firearms, gun charges were filed against some of the protestors.

Four people on site died of natural causes (stroke, heart attack) including Officer Brian Sicknik who was said to have been attacked by a rioter with a fire extinguisher. Outrage over this policeman's death and no accounting for the true fact that he went home from the Capitol Hill event and died the next day—of natural causes (multiple strokes). Grudgingly, the *Washington Post* and the *New York Times* finally admitted that fact. Indisputable fact: none of the five deaths on that day were directly brought about by the protestors.

It requires no stretch of reason to deduce that the Democratic Party absolutely needs to keep shouting from the rooftops that January 6 was a violent insurrection, an example of domestic terrorism. The president and the House majority leader have compared it to the Japanese attack on Pearl Harbor, the 9/11 bombings, and even the Civil War.

Meanwhile, another fact easily apparent: the one hundred plus people arrested on January 6 are still in prison, many in solitary confinement, and all have been denied a speedy trial. The press guessed that they would all be charged with criminal sedition, but many are just being charged with trespassing—curiouser and curiouser. I believe Roger Kimball has made his case.

BACK TO THE 2020 SUMMER RIOTS: HOW THEY WERE HANDLED

The mainstream press deserves as high a level of blame as the government officials who accepted the violence as justified. The press blatantly ignored the violence to present a fraudulent picture of peaceful protests.

And what of our medical knights in masked armor, the twelve hundred doctors and health care people who signed a public statement approving the thousands demonstrating in the city streets, justifying the risky behavior that would spread the virus? These medical people are part of the same establishment that demanded we must all stay in lockdown, no attending funerals or church services or anything bringing people together—except protests.[1]

On to the destruction of public monuments and buildings. The public display of utter ignorance on the part of the destructive actors is disheartening. To tear down the statue of Black abolitionist Frederick Douglas? Of Ulysses S. Grant who led the Union Army in the war to end slavery, a man who never owned slaves? In Philadelphia a group of Italian Americans stood defending the statue of Christopher Columbus from rioters. After the statue was torn down, the mayor ordered the defending citizens to be arrested, not the rioters.

On December 20, 2020, a truly "woke" group of students protested the name of their school—Abraham Lincoln High School in San Francisco. They demanded that its name be changed, saying that Lincoln really didn't show that "black lives mattered that much to him." In spite of protests on social media, the school board voted on January 26 to approve the change.

They had until April 2020 to come up with a new name. One may reasonably wonder at the poor quality of the teaching of U.S. history in the San Francisco schools that its students would reveal such abysmal ignorance.[2]

On June 28, 2020, a middle-aged couple in St. Louis, Missouri, Mark and Patricia McCloskey, stood in front of their home holding guns to deter a group of protesters who had broken through a gate to their little street of private homes. The couple had called the police when they saw the threat to their home. The police advised them to leave the house. Next, they called the governor's office and were told he could do nothing. The protesters finally departed.

These two people were promptly accused by the authorities of making threatening gestures and had to defend themselves in court. Both had gun carry licenses and their guns were not loaded. We saw this scene on television news and must ask ourselves how public officials can stand tall and try to justify punishing these two people for defending their home but not the invaders who appeared bent on inflicting damage to this home and neighborhood.

On June 17, 2021, the McCloskeys appeared in court, agreed to pay a $3,000 fine, and gave up the guns they were legally entitled to own. The case against them rested on the accusation that they had put the protesters in danger by pointing their guns at the crowd. Outside the courtroom, Mark McCloskey agreed that they put the protesters in danger: "That's what guns are for, and I'd do it again any time the mob approaches me."[3]

WHITE PRIVILEGE EXISTENCE CODIFIED

Companion essays in this volume point out that the harm of identity politics, the erosion of free speech, and other examples of cultural changes are threatening to our democracy, and that they are intensifying. Since the death of George Floyd, the newly invigorated Black Lives Matter movement and the entire anti-racism movement now pose even greater danger to our country. They are not pushing for equality of opportunity. It is a Jacobin/Marxist revolutionary project to frighten and demean the United States, to bring us all to our knees. The aim is to destroy "White Privilege."

How quickly and cravenly the political leaders on the left and leaders of large corporations have caved, swearing allegiance to Black Lives Matter and accepting the poisonous notion that the United States is a country deeply racist since before its establishment (see the *1619* project of the *New York Times*)[4]. This deeply flawed narrative has been dismissed by many respected historians. The *1619* project paints all Whites as guilty of creating a country that sustains structural and systemic racism and White privilege. A detailed analysis follows in the essay on critical race theory.

This view of race is not a subject for public debate as anyone who disagrees is immediately labeled a racist and is subjected to a variety of punishments up to and including dismissal from employment. It is important to note that there are a few very brave academics who challenge this orthodoxy of thinking on race.

One such person is Peter Wood, president of the National Association of Scholars, whose new book, *The 1620 Project: A Critical Response to the 1619 Project*, has received a measure of critical acclaim and dozens of interviews for the author, though the *New York Times* fails to recognize or review it. Wood's project is examined at length in the essay that follows.

But for a few courageous opinion writers such as Heather MacDonald, Rich Lowry, Robert L. Woodson, Sr., and Jason L. Riley, few dare to express different opinions. Certainly not our titans of large corporations, the elites of Silicon Valley, Wall Street, and Hollywood. The heads of Google, Facebook, Apple, Disney, and their ilk carp daily on this subject. We, like our betters, must grovel, kneel, and accept guilt, or at the least put a Black Lives Matter sign on our lawns.

And then what? Is it enough to keep spending public and private funds to pay the race hustlers to give us more sensitivity training, more anti-racism workshops? By sound estimation, Robin DiAngelo, the high priestess of anti-racism corporate training sessions, is earning millions for promoting this deep guilt in American people.

Has Black Lives Matter yet delineated a public policy or program for expiating the monstrous guilt? If such a program has been formulated, it has not yet been publicly announced—leaving all Whites in limbo. Where is the path to redemption?

A LITTLE *AIDE MEMOIR* FOR OUR "WOKE" KINDRED

Young people of this millennium, the so-called "Y" and "Z" generations, may not be fully attuned to the decades-long efforts to improve the prospects for the Black community since the end of World War II—*Brown v. Board of Education* in 1954 to desegregate the public schools; the *Civil Rights Act of 1964*; and the *Voting Rights Act of 1965* to finally make those rights real. The enormous financial and social efforts invested in raising educational and employment opportunities for the Black community have had long-lasting, positive effects for millions of people.

Over the last fifty years, a Black middle class and a professional class have emerged, with affirmative action in college admissions and in awarding of contracts playing a crucial part in assuring the growth. A significant event was the Black migration from the rural south to the industrial north, from 1915 to 1970, a population movement that dramatically changed the outcomes for families to gain work and education opportunities never available to them in the south.

Black leaders attaining success led to these improvements in educational and economic progress: for example, secretaries of state Colin Powell and Condaleeza Rice; Robert Woodson, business leader and philanthropist; scholars John McWhorter at Columbia, Thomas Sowell and Shelby Steele at Stanford, Ward Connerly at Berkeley, Randall Kennedy at Harvard Law School, and Glenn C. Loury at Brown University.

At the highest levels of government and the judiciary, we had Supreme Court justices Thurgood Marshall and Clarence Thomas; and Dr. Ben Carson, head of Health and Human Services. Substantial numbers of elected Black mayors, governors, representatives, and senators are prominently represented in various levels of government. Most impressive of all, we had our first Black president of the United States, Barack Obama. It is useful to note that all of these elected officials up to the president were elected by majorities of White voters.

During those same years of civil rights activity, the heavy hand of the federal government, including President Lyndon Johnson and his Great Society, began concentrated efforts on providing more and more funding for welfare plans that, unintentionally, weakened the Black community.

These policies promoted the following self-defeating behaviors: the breakdown of the Black family; out of wedlock births (70 percent in 2020), with no responsibility on fathers to support families; demeaning the work ethic and the value of education as "white ways"; a culture glorifying antisocial behavior; gangs; blaming of everything on Whites; and no responsibility on Blacks for their own acts.

PROFESSOR GLENN C. LOURY INTUITED THE PROBLEM DECADES AGO

Four decades ago, Glenn C. Loury became the first Black tenured professor of economics in Harvard's history. He is noted over his career for his iconoclastic ideas about race and for his very sharp cultural criticism. In 1984 he published an article in *The New Republic*, "A New American Dilemma."[5] In a few sentences he summarized the failures in the Black community over the twenty years of intense efforts, the Great Society programs most noteworthy. His analysis of the problems at that time reveal the disappointing results evident today, that the Black community has not achieved the anticipated uniform improvements.

What Loury said in 1984 reflected the research reported by the sociologists James Coleman and Daniel Patrick Moynihan, whose conclusions about the causes of Black poverty were routinely criticized. Loury wrote, "[T]he social disorganization among poor blacks, the lagging academic performance of black students, the disturbingly high rate of black crime, the alarming increase in the early unwed pregnancies among blacks now loom as the primary obstacles to progress."[6]

Before his article was published, Loury met in Washington, DC, with an urban coalition and civil rights leaders where he presented the ideas in his forthcoming *New Republic* article. He expected that he might receive some measure of agreement with his ideas, but he suffered a deep disappointment. His words were not what the Black leaders wanted to hear. Their general response was to disagree with what he said and to condemn it as reactionary talk that would only give comfort to the enemy.

Apparently, they had imbibed the elixir of condemning any criticism of Black behavior as "blaming the victim." That ancient, defensive trope still holds sway with many leaders of any race today. Some might deem it a marvel that we are still making the same excuses for self-defeating behaviors when in the years since 1984 so much success has been recorded in the Black community.

There seems to be a heavy curtain drawn between the two groups: the numbers who have worked hard to rise above poverty, through education, military service, special mentoring, taking advantage of whatever breaks came their way; and those who are mired in the same circumstances described by Loury in his 1984 piece, a terribly sad plight.

Voices of responsible, successful Black leaders are not popular with the progressive, "woke" left. Race baiters have made a career of shaking down corporations and government—the most visible example being Al Sharpton. His various career moves of promoting false narratives for profit and to demonize non-Blacks (Tawana Brawley incident, etc.) did not discourage the Obama administration from making him an invited guest to the White House.

In July 2020, the honorable Smithsonian Institution's National Museum of African American History published an infographic on its website titled "Aspects and Assumptions of Whiteness and White Culture in the United States." The purported goal of this document was to make clear how these elements of our daily life in the United States, the models we consider standard practice in our country have been promoted by White dominant culture and—"because White people still hold most of the power in America—they have been internalized by all, including people of color" (see figure 6.01).

This document, placed online by the Smithsonian as social practices to be rejected because of their "Whiteness," is truly revealing of a warped mind set. It begs to be reprinted here in its entirety:

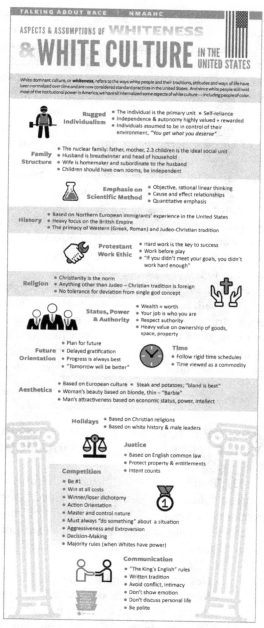

ASPECTS & ASSUMPTIONS OF **WHITENESS**

& WHITE CULTURE IN THE UNITED STATES

White dominant culture, or **whiteness**, refers to the ways white people and their traditions, attitudes and ways of life have been normalized over time and are now considered standard practices in the United States. And since white people still hold most of the institutional power in America, we have all internalized some aspects of white culture — including people of color.

Rugged Individualism
- The individual is the primary unit • Self-reliance
- Independence & autonomy highly valued + rewarded
- Individuals assumed to be in control of their environment, *"You get what you deserve"*

Family Structure
- The nuclear family: father, mother, 2.3 children is the ideal social unit
- Husband is breadwinner and head of household
- Wife is homemaker and subordinate to the husband
- Children should have own rooms, be independent

Emphasis on Scientific Method
- Objective, rational linear thinking
- Cause and effect relationships
- Quantitative emphasis

History
- Based on Northern European immigrants' experience in the United States
- Heavy focus on the British Empire
- The primacy of Western (Greek, Roman) and Judeo-Christian tradition

Protestant Work Ethic
- Hard work is the key to success
- Work before play
- "If you didn't meet your goals, you didn't work hard enough"

Religion
- Christianity is the norm
- Anything other than Judeo – Christian tradition is foreign
- No tolerance for deviation from single god concept

Status, Power & Authority
- Wealth = worth
- Your job is who you are
- Respect authority
- Heavy value on ownership of goods, space, property

Future Orientation
- Plan for future
- Delayed gratification
- Progress is always best
- "Tomorrow will be better"

Time
- Follow rigid time schedules
- Time viewed as a commodity

Aesthetics
- Based on European culture • Steak and potatoes; "bland is best"
- Woman's beauty based on blonde, thin – "Barbie"
- Man's attractiveness based on economic status, power, intellect

Holidays
- Based on Christian religions
- Based on white history & male leaders

Justice
- Based on English common law
- Protect property & entitlements
- Intent counts

Competition
- Be #1
- Win at all costs
- Winner/loser dichotomy
- Action Orientation
- Master and control nature
- Must always "do something" about a situation
- Aggressiveness and Extroversion
- Decision-Making
- Majority rules (when Whites have power)

Communication
- "The King's English" rules
- Written tradition
- Avoid conflict, intimacy
- Don't show emotion
- Don't discuss personal life
- Be polite

Figure 6.01: Aspects & Assumptions of Whiteness & White Culture in the United States. Image: ©2020 NMAAHC, All Rights Reserved. Data Source: "Some Aspects and Assumptions of White Culture in the United States," by Judith H. Katz, ©1990. The Kaleel Jamison Consulting Group, Inc. All Rights Reserved.

A clear animus is displayed in this chart against societal norms that were, until recently, considered worthwhile. It is a challenge to any rational, even minimally educated adult to imagine that rejecting these so-called "White" standards would empower the Black community. The awful "White" behaviors to be rejected include the work ethic, promptness, the two-parent family, education, religion, willingness to compete/rugged individualism, and objective rational scientific thinking. Personally, as a member of an immigrant family of poverty in my childhood, I firmly believe my siblings and I attained various degrees of success because we adopted the "White" practices outlined above.

Soon after some tens of thousands of viewers had accessed the Smithsonian chart, a backlash emerged, and the chart was erased from the museum website.

Since 2020, the anti-racism virus has infected the whole country at a fever pitch, especially in elite centers of higher education such as my hometown of Amherst, Massachusetts. We must all read *White Fragility* (DiAngelo 2018) and *Caste* (Wilkerson 2020), and *How to Be an Anti-Racist* (Kendi 2020)—there must be no limit to the practice of self-loathing.

Even if one were to acknowledge the rightness of the anti-racism movement, is this a healthy path for improving the plight of Black Americans and curing the endemic/structural racism of the White community? Rather than continuing with readings of the majority voices fulminating in this vein, it is time to find some Black voices of high intellectual acuity who pose very different and well-documented views on the subject of racial inequality in America.

PROFESSOR LOURY SPEAKS OUT: A STRONG VOICE FOR RESPONSIBLE DIALOGUE

On February 8, 2021, Professor Glenn C. Loury of Brown University delivered a guest lecture at the University of Colorado titled "Unspeakable Truths about Racial Inequality in America." He took on himself the formidable task of both speaking for his people (Black Americans) and examining and reporting the truth of racial inequality and the threat of "cancel culture" in an open, public debate.

Short of copying Professor Loury's entire speech, I summarize here the major points he puts forward and, as was once said in a famous Bette Davis movie, "Fasten your seat belts; we're in for a bumpy ride."

There is an honest dilemma among Black intellectuals in representing the racial inequality issue: should they emphasize mainly the positives, the good, law-abiding African Americans who form the majority, to bring respectability and dignity to the community? Or should they focus instead on the historical causes of the over-representation of young Black men in the crime and prison statistics, of the poverty and low educational achievements?

Loury admits he cannot know all the answers but will put forward what he has studied and learned to date that may clarify the issues. He rejects the path of attributing it all to "White supremacy." He also suggests that it's time for those so-called "White intellectuals" to join the public dialogue, to stop giving all their public effort to repeating anti-racist slogans.

LOURY'S SEVEN UNSPEAKABLE TRUTHS

Unspeakable Truth #1: Downplaying Behavioral Disparities by Race Is Actually a "Bluff"

The most essential element in the racial differences in achievement and the old notion of "upward mobility" that so many Blacks are not experiencing can be partly blamed on behavioral norms in the Black community. The 1966 publication of the Coleman Report explored racial differences in educational achievement. That report was immediately disparaged and accused of "blaming the victim."[7]

Over fifty years, any claim that a segment of the Black community follows self-defeating behaviors is immediately shouted down. Today, more than ever, anyone daring to make such a statement is labeled a racist. Loury goes further to say that while left-leaning activists routinely credit "White supremacy" and "implicit bias" as the true causes of Black disadvantage, they are really posing a bluff. Anyone responding who dares to disagree will be "canceled," that is, shamed publicly or even fired from their place of employment.

He suggests instead that people are not being arrested, convicted, and sent to jail because of their race. Those in prison are principally there because they've committed criminal acts and a large percentage of their victims are other Blacks, a terrible fact that will be explored with statistical data later in this essay.

A large impediment to educational achievement in the Black community is not racism but "behavior, with cultural patterns, with what peer groups value, with how people spend their time, with what they identify as being critical to their own self-respect."[8] Bearing children out of wedlock—without husbands, to be precise—is the practice of 70 percent of black women today. It may be the most corrosive, self-damaging development for the decimating of the Black family since the 1960s. These same decades brought the greatest strides in ending segregation and promoting equal rights, yet we still have the disparities in educational success and upward mobility in the black community.

A Local Massachusetts Example

My professional work in educational research and advocacy over forty years covers not only a focus on immigrant children but on the achievements of minority groups. For ten years, I was an administrator in the Newton, Massachusetts, public schools, a wealthy community outside Boston that prides itself equally on its high standards for student success and on its special efforts on behalf of minority students.

The METCO program, introduced in 1966, allowed families in Boston's Black community to send their children to kindergarten or first grade in the suburban districts. These children were provided transportation and enrolled in the schools of towns like Brookline, Newton, Concord, from kindergarten through twelfth grade. The program is still in effect to this day. It has proved highly successful for the students from Boston, a high percentage of whom graduate from high school and many of whom go on to college.

However, Newton administrators were made cognizant of an uncomfortable truth: the local Black students, born and bred in Newton in middle-class families with professional parents, were not achieving academic success at the level of the METCO kids from low-status Boston families. It was a real struggle to understand the fact that children from families of low-income, working-class parents with little schooling could do so well.

Two crucial factors occurred to us at the time: Those Boston parents had high aspirations and a willingness to grasp an opportunity presented to them. They also believed that enrolling their children in better schools would give them a breakout opportunity. In spite of the long travels each day on the school bus and having to adapt to new schools farther from their homes, the children were given the parental support and encouragement to get their education in the suburbs.

How to account for the less admirable academic performance of the Black students born and raised in middle-class privilege? In the late 1980s, Newton enlisted a local consulting firm to examine the data, conduct interviews to explain the underperformance of this group, provide teacher training workshops, and propose some remedies. It was a project of low value that produced very few hard conclusions and was quietly buried.[9]

Back to Professor Loury

When considering the group on the opposite side of the achievement gap, Asian-Americans, our left-leaning friends can hardly bear to acknowledge what stares them right straight in the face. The preponderance of proof for the academic excellence of such a large percentage of Asian American children is directly attributable to cultural patterns of this community.

Their families engage in behavior and follow disciplines that impress on their children the value of hard work, studying, and respect for learning. It is the families that make the accomplishments of their children possible and not any innate benefit from birth. Simple and indisputable as this is, I must and will say it: behavior matters more than race.

Unspeakable Truth #2: Structural Racism Isn't an Explanation, It's an Empty Category and Unspeakable Truth #3: We Must Put the Police Killing of Black Americans in Perspective

These two truths are combined since they both focus on the explanations for the criminal activity and incarceration of young Black men and the killings of Black Americans. For Loury, "structural racism" is an empty political term that explains nothing. It is a call to solidarity, to attribute the higher proportion of Blacks in prison to this ill-defined term and to nothing else. Anyone who dares to voice the opposite—that skin color is not the only reason for racial disparities; there are multiple causes—is in trouble.

Loury provides information on police killings of Black Americans from an impeccable source, the *Washington Post* data base, which tracks all police killings. The numbers are these:

- 1,200 fatal shootings by police in the United States each year
- 300 of that number are blacks—25 percent of the total, but not all are unarmed innocents, most are engaged in crimes
- there is a racial disparity since Blacks make up 13 percent of the country's population, but this is explained by the fact that Blacks participate in criminal activity at a much higher level
- far more Whites than Blacks are killed by the police every year

To put these figures in perspective: 17,000 homicides occur in the United States every year and nearly half are committed by Blacks. According to Loury's analysis, for every Black killed by the police, more than twenty-five Blacks are killed by other Blacks.

These facts do not make their way into headlines in the mainstream press or receive any attention from good White journalists. White silence is almost universal as the fear of being "canceled" is real. But why is Black Lives Matter missing in action as far as publicly caring for the plight of Black victims of Black crime?

All the rhetoric in the months since George Floyd was killed would have us believe that Blacks are routinely killed by White police and are only sentenced to prison on racist grounds. These beliefs are demonstrably untrue and must be refuted.

On February 26, 2021, a perfect proof for Professor Loury's contentions appeared in the local Florida newspaper, the *Palm Beach Post*, "Study: Black Men, Boys More Likely Gun Victims." This article states its main conclusion: Black men and teens made up a third of homicide victims in 2019, according to the Centers for Disease Control (CDC) new study, "A Public Health Crisis in the Making."[10]

There is much alarming data on the percentage of Blacks gunned down across the country, figures for men/women, increases in these tragic killings, but one set of facts is entirely missing in this Centers for Disease Control study: Who are the perpetrators of these gun crimes? Who is doing the shooting? Not a word on the race of the killers.

Unspeakable Truth #4: The Dark Side of the "White Fragility" Blame Game

Now is the time to look at both sides of the blame game and consider this: in the physical world, every action produces a reaction. Loury puts it very well: "I wonder if the 'white-guilt' and 'white-apologia' and 'white-privilege' view of the world cannot exist except to give birth to a 'white pride' backlash, even if the latter is seldom expressed overtly—it being politically incorrect to do so."[11]

Loury asks, "How can we make 'whiteness' into a site of unrelenting moral indictment without also occasioning it to become the basis of pride, of identity and, ultimately, of self-affirmation? . . . Promoting anti-whiteness (and Black Lives Matter often seems to flirt with this) may cause one to reap what one sows in a backlash of pro-whiteness."[12] From many conversations with liberal colleagues and friends, this idea has not yet entered their minds.

Loury proposes instead that the best thinking for today is to return to the glorious precepts of Mahatma Gandhi and Martin Luther King, Jr., that we put aside race and concentrate on our common humanity. President John F. Kennedy gave our world a thought on our humanity back in the early 1960s when he was negotiating bilateral nuclear disarmament with the Soviet Union: "In the final analysis, our most basic common link is that we all inhabit this small planet. We all breathe the same air. We all cherish our children's future. And we are all mortal."[13]

Unspeakable Truth #5: Black Fragility Infantilizes Blacks

There is an assumption of Black fragility in the anti-racism arguments. Blacks are treated as so weak that they cannot be disagreed with, criticized, or asked anything, lest they be irreparably harmed. There is a tacit understanding then, that Blacks are not accountable for what they do as racism entirely controls their lives.

There is also an illogic in the basic anti-racism ideology. If we assume White Americans to be systemically racist, and Whites are bludgeoned daily to accept this accusation, how can we then turn around and demand that Whites save Blacks from this racism?

How can Whites be expected to rise to a decent moral standard and start delivering Blacks from the consequences of racism? Are we saying then that Blacks cannot act for themselves, that we must wait for Whites to save them, but that there's little hope that those awful White racists will do it? Is this circular reasoning or is something eluding us?

Unspeakable Truths #6 and #7: On Achieving "True Equality" for Black Americans

Loury reminds us that Black Americans worked mightily after the end of slavery and in the face of tremendous Jim Crow obstacles to begin their own emancipation. Within fifty years they raised their literacy level from zero to the mass population's capacity to read. The Black family with its roots in the Black church was a powerful force for raising themselves, educating their children, acquiring work skills, and finally creating the basis for the civil rights movement that changed the country and our politics.

The upward trajectory of achievement in the Black community is rightly due to the enormous efforts of Blacks who, until the late 1960s, relied mostly on themselves and their own community. Isabel Wilkerson produced an eloquent study of the Black migration from southern rural poverty to the industrial north in the period from 1915 to the 1970s, *The Warmth of Other Suns* (2010). She is an eminent Black journalist, honored and highly respected in academic circles.

From the high peak of one hundred years of striving after emancipation, the insidious effects of well-intentioned social programs began to erode the Black family and community, in part due to government support of self-defeating behavior. It has become commonplace since then, and more so in the recent past, to ridicule such values as taking responsibility for one's own life and not constantly blaming one's failures on racism.

The reality is that life is not fair, but that's the way of the world. There is no utopia for Whites or Blacks, and we must each work to make the best of our own lives. The Greek word "utopia" means "nowhere."

The final unspeakable truth Loury states, with great force and in defiance of "cancel culture," is this:

[I]f we want to be truly equal then we must realize that White people cannot give us equality. We actually have to earn equal status . . .. I am on the side of Black people here. But I feel obliged to report that equality of dignity, of standing, of honor, of security in one's position in society, of being able to command the respect of others—this is not something that can be handed over. Rather, it is something that one has to wrest from a cruel and indifferent world with hard work, with our bare hands, inspired by the example of our enslaved and newly freed ancestors. We have to make ourselves equal. No one can do it for us."[14]

Thus ends the summation of the brave, noble ideas of a very courageous Black American. Thankfully, Professor Glenn Loury is not alone in taking a very visible public stance on race issues in twenty-first century America. Time to focus briefly now on an arena of tremendous importance: the shift from equality to equity as the most urgent social goal.

THE TRANSITION FROM EQUALITY TO EQUITY: SHELBY STEELE AND CHARLES LIPSON

The basic difference between equality and equity may be stated simply as the difference between equal treatment and equal outcomes. There is a deep ravine between these two concepts. Equality is in the bedrock of our founding documents as a nation, the belief that all men are created equal. The civil rights movement of the 1960s relied on this concept and called for equal treatment under the law for all, equal opportunity and equal standards for judging behavior.

The new equity concept is about nothing but outcomes and discrimination in favor of certain groups if their performance does not match other groups. Professor Shelby Steele said, in a February 13–14, 2021, interview published in the *Wall Street Journal* that "America has made more moral progress in the last 60 years regarding race than any nation, country, or civilization in history."[15]

In an op-ed piece on March 5, 2021, also in the *Wall Street Journal*, emeritus professor of political science at the University of Chicago, Charles Lipson, takes issue with the "equity" campaign as a "mandate to discriminate." He is unalterably opposed to unequal treatment, of giving special benefits to adults today because of the unfair treatment of earlier generations or because of a disadvantaged childhood.[16]

Unequal benefits for certain groups are losing popular support and are being renamed. "Quotas" were restyled as "affirmative action" for a while, giving special benefits to some groups to achieve desired outcomes. Now, according to Lipson, even the term "affirmative action" has become toxic, and the same old idea is now labeled "equity." At the end of his piece, Lipson makes a tough call: "Since the ultimate goal is achieving equal outcomes, these evasions raise the hardest question of all. Isn't equity just a new brand name for the oldest program of achieving equal outcomes? Its name is socialism."[17]

PRINCETON UNIVERSITY ACCUSED: AMHERST COLLEGE RUSHES TO THE DEFENSE

In March 2020, just before the COVID-19 pandemic obliterated most other news topics, Princeton University president Christopher L. Eisgruber released a letter to the public addressing racism throughout the university's history and the steps it would take to improve itself. The letter states that "Princeton for most of its history, intentionally and systemically, excluded people of color, women, Jews, and other minorities."[18] Eisgruber claims that although diversity is now a documented fact at the University, "systemic racism still persists at Princeton and in society at large."[19]

The new anti-racism has been ramping up the encouragement of guilty pleas from all the most "left-leaning" entities. Princeton happened to be one of the first and most prominent institutions to accuse itself, not only for past actions of discrimination but to acknowledge that this stuff is still going on. What had not been anticipated by President Eisgruber is that the Department of Education in Washington would take him at his word. He'd led the university to be hoisted by its own petard!

The basic problem, clearly enunciated by Secretary of Education Betsy DeVos, is that every year when universities apply for federal funds, they submit documents confirming non-discrimination assurances. Princeton is to be investigated for falsely alleging that there is no discrimination at the university, while their own public statements say exactly the opposite. The investigation may lead to a demand for the university to return some of its federal funds.

Amherst College President Biddy Martin promptly took a leading role in a campaign to protest the action against Princeton. A letter describing the Education Department's unconscionable investigation is signed by all the great and the good presidents, at the likes of Yale, Harvard, Williams, Wesleyan, and others.

The threat of federal funds being taken back by the federal government is proclaimed to be too harsh. The leaders agree that racism continues to affect the country and to be a problem at their own educational institutions. Surely it is outrageous that the government would try to punish Princeton for addressing past racism.

But that is not the true issue. The true cause for government action is the fact that if the Education Department is to take Princeton at its word, they've been lying to the government in their documents applying for funding. Why should the feds *not* launch a fact-finding investigation?

As is sometimes the case with high visibility efforts to crack down on public funding misdeeds, by the time the investigative machinery gets cranked up, there is a change of administration in our nation's capital. Since the all-government change in January 2021, with the Democrats gaining the White House and effective control of the Senate and the House of Representatives, the investigation will probably not be heard of again.

Amherst College President Biddy Martin, however, now announces that they have cleaned up their act on the discrimination issue. The college is exonerated of the original sin of exclusivity by trumpeting the new reality that "a school once known as a bastion of wealthy, white (and, for over 150 years, male) students has an incoming class this September of 2021 in which about 51 percent of the U.S. students identify as people of color."[20]

The virtuous fact of such an inordinately high enrollment of what Amherst now calls "domestic people of color" may register as strangely out of step with the conventional thinking of proportionate representations of Whites and people of color (POC). According to the most recent census, if one can even believe the government's figures, Whites account for close to 70 percent of the country.

Is it possible that we are over-counting the numbers in each defined POC group, or that the descriptors for each group have grown so complex that people assign themselves to more than one category, thereby skewing the count?

THE PERFECT STORM: SMITH COLLEGE BECOMES FIRST AMONG ELITE COLLEGES TO BE EXPOSED BY THE *NEW YORK TIMES*

This development is an irresistibly perfect story that distills all the dominant forces in academia today. It contains every element of the current ideology of Black oppression and White fragility at our most prestigious institutions of *soi-disant* "higher education." The delicious irony of being exposed by the *New York Times* in a front-page feature on February 25, 2021—one cannot conceive of a more just and timely publication to lift the lid on this malodorous swamp and to allow the wider public to inhale the noxious fumes.

It is a combination of the Communist show trials in the USSR of the Cold War era and the Senator Joe McCarthy anti-Communist witch hunts in our own country, two sides of the same coin, the destruction of unorthodox thinking. It also happens to reveal the new, unlovely aspect of a prestigious women's college and the machinations that go on behind the scenes.

The first year of the COVID-19 pandemic—March 2020 to March 2021, to be exact—locked us down. Then it brought us the nightly rioting in several U.S. cities to express public outrage against our national racism that fosters the killings of Black men by White police. Black Lives Matter rose to its highest peak of power, promoting its "defund the police" creed, and lending support to the rioters.

In recent years, a string of *mea culpa* statements has been announced by the presidents of elite institutions, all lamenting to the world how terribly and unequally they had treated their minority students. An obligatory orgy of regretful feelings confessed with promises of curative steps to be taken— more funding for anti-racist programs; more training for faculty, staff, and administrators; and more attention to the expressions of minority students and more catering to their sensitivities.

Ideally, everyone interested in this revelation about Smith College should get the article by Michael Powell and read it first-hand for full effect. A summary of the high points of this story is to reveal two main themes: the unreasonable, wrongful actions of administrators at Smith; and the foul ugliness of mounting a racist accusation that is false. The racist incident did not happen as described but was manufactured for the ego gratification and self-promotion of the accuser.

The outcome of this false accusation is the damage to people who have committed no sin, who are forced into "reeducation" sessions, made to apologize, and are shamed in the Northampton community where they have resided for decades. They are, in effect, punished for "working while White," to assuage the feelings of the student who feels victimized for "eating while Black."

Let's go to the details of this illustrative morality tale at Smith College. On July 31, 2018, Oumou Kanoute, a Smith College student working on campus for the summer, went into Tyler House dorm cafeteria to get lunch. Ms. Jackie Blair, a cafeteria employee, mentioned to Ms. Kanoute that the cafeteria was closed to students for the summer as it was reserved for a children's day camp.

Ms. Kanoute took her lunch to the lounge of the building closed for the summer where she was noticed by a college janitor. A thirty-five-year employee of the college, he knew better than to approach the student but followed the rules and called security. The elderly security man recognized the student, apologized for bothering her, and informed her of the building rule in a short conversation, which the student recorded.

That evening Ms. Kanoute began the rewriting of history in her Facebook post where she stated her outrage that people questioned why she was at Smith and her existence as a woman of color. Thus, that brief exchange with the security guard was distorted out of all recognition. The accusations she added included being "misgendered" as the janitor couldn't tell if it was a man or a woman sitting in the shadows; that she had a "meltdown" when she feared the security guard might be carrying a weapon; and that she was suffering a yearlong "pattern of discrimination."

Smith College president McCartney, it must be noted, publicly apologized to the student immediately on the appearance of the Facebook post before any investigation was even initiated. She then hired a law firm noted for its experience in discrimination cases, and they produced a thirty-five-page report for the college in fall of 2018. Their findings were as follows:

- there was no persuasive evidence of bias as claimed by the student;
- Ms. Blair, the cafeteria worker and the janitor who called security were cleared of any act of discrimination;
- Smith security police are unarmed; and
- there was nothing to support the claim by Ms. Kanoute that she experienced a year of discrimination.

So, the facts are that Ms. Kanoute ramped up the false charges publicly and was supported by the ACLU and the entire Smith College community. She became a national celebrity of the downtrodden. Additionally, when Ms. Kanoute demanded that a separate dormitory for Black students be established, her recommendation was rapidly granted.

How were the innocent workers treated by our betters at Smith? Were they issued an apology for the "misunderstandings"? No, sir. The janitor was put on paid leave. Ms. Blair was assigned to another dormitory than the one she had worked in for years. The workers were scapegoated, forced to sit in training sessions where they were bullied about childhood and family experiences about race, the whole White fragility playbook.

Ms. Blair suffered the most as her physical health problems were exacerbated by the stress of being labeled a racist in the college community, losing her job at the college, and not being able to get hired elsewhere as the label apparently spread around town.

One other departure from Smith College, following the Kanoute extravaganza, made the local news. In February 2021, Jodi Shaw, a college administrator and Smith graduate, resigned her position on the grounds that Smith had become a "racially hostile environment." We should note that Ms. Shaw is not a "person of color."

President McCartney has much to answer for as she has demonstrated on half a dozen occasions in recent years that she has no backbone and will cave to any demand by any student or group no matter how unwarranted, if it has to do with race (see chapter 4, "Freedom of Speech"). The infuriating aspect of this Smith tale is that it is not at all unusual. The toxic ideology entrenched at Smith is the norm at similar institutions.

What of Ms. Kanoute, the New York–raised woman, daughter of a family that moved to the United States from Mali, what career is she pursuing these days? She is an activist on various projects related to medical care disparities between Whites and Blacks, a defender of women's rights to abortion, and is currently a research assistant in the Columbia University Graduate School of Social Work. Post Smith College, her online identity reveals her concentration strongly focuses on matters of race.

The ideal of an integrated, equal society we worked so hard for in my earlier professional years is totally eclipsed by the new racial segregation demanded by students like Ms. Kanoute. To speak against the accepted norms at Smith would be to put one's moral capital and one's livelihood at risk. One lone comment by a faculty member is quoted in the *New York Times* article, that of economics professor James Miller: "My perception is that if you're on the wrong side of issues of identity politics, you're not just mistaken, you're evil."[21]

On March 22, 2021, a letter was sent to Smith College President Kathleen McCartney by Robert L. Woodson, Sr., and forty-four co-signers, objecting to the treatment of the college workers. It read in part,

> We, the undersigned, are writing as Black Americans to express our outrage at the treatment of the service workers of Smith College in light of the incident of alleged racial profiling that occurred in the summer of 2018. Before investigating the facts, Smith College assumed that every one of the people who prepare its food and clean its facilities was guilty of the vile sin of racism and forced them to publicly "cleanse" themselves through a series of humiliating exercises in order to keep their jobs. . . . Smith College offered no public apology to the falsely accused and merely doubled down on the shaming of its most vulnerable employees.[22]

That an organization of Black leaders in American professions, businesses, and education would take up the cause of White service workers merits profound appreciation. The plea that the college extend an apology to the workers, stop inflicting "anti-bias" training, and even compensate them for the harm they suffered—those suggestions went entirely unheeded.

To zero in on where and why incidents such as the one at Smith occur, *New York Times* columnist Bret Stephens poses a few provocative questions. He asks, "Why is it that racial tensions keep boiling over at the most progressive-minded institutions? Why does the embrace of social justice pedagogy seem to go hand in hand with deteriorating racial relations?"[23]

Fair questions. Stephens suggests three reasons. Since college students are being fed a steady diet of critical race theory and a lot of gender/sex/race ideology, they begin to take it seriously. Another reason may simply be that it is becoming obvious that those who claim they are being offended or harassed get a lot of attention and sympathy, and it could well encourage others to jump on this bandwagon.

But Stephens guesses that the strongest reason may be that the new progressive, far left strategy is to instill guilt in good White liberals. "Restorative justice" is not a true liberal agenda. It is the reigning ideology today on college campuses—divisive, judgmental, unforgiving. This discordant path of human relations will not subside until college leaders wake up and start taking strongly reasoned stands to counteract it, to take us out of the morass of race, race, and nothing counts but race.

THE VIRTUOUS ARE TOO CREDULOUS

What of the ordinary folks in a typical college town such as Amherst, not the *professoriat*? It seems that even "the butcher, the baker, the candle-stick maker" in this academic community have internalized the racism pathology.

In recent months, columns in the local newspaper provide a few representative examples of how the thinking goes in Western Massachusetts. The arguments explaining our sins are getting more and more complex and weird. One column proposes two comparable scenarios: going to the dentist and vowing to brush and floss our teeth, but gradually neglecting those two tasks as time goes on; or proclaiming a commitment to fighting racism and then lazily forgetting the promise and taking no actions. It requires quite a stretch to make these two behaviors comparable.[24]

Another day, a local pastor titles her column in the same newspaper, "Are We an Enclave of 'Nice Racists'?"[25] The good pastor was shocked to learn that the most famous diversity trainer in the United States, Robin DiAngelo, has named Northampton, Massachusetts, "a town full of white progressives." And that term is employed as a pejorative. The title of DiAngelo's new book is enough to make this category as clear as can be: *Nice Racism: How Progressive White People Perpetuate Racial Harm.*[26]

Once again, no matter how sensitive, how committed, and how active a White person in this town may be in racial matters, it means nothing. It is judged by Ms. DiAngelo to be insufficient. The pastor in Northampton accepts this judgment, that her skin color is the only thing that counts, and it counts against her, no matter her willingness to accept guilt. Self-criticism is a good thing, but it should be balanced by a healthy degree of self-awareness.

ARMED INSURRECTION? OR A
WEEKEND IN THE COUNTRY?

In rural western Massachusetts on the eve of the 2021 July 4th holiday cel-
ebration, all planned public observances veered sharply away from readings
of the Declaration of Independence or marching bands with patriotic songs.
This year many towns revamped their town events to feature readings from
African American leaders instead, who spoke passionate, accusatory words.
But in the vicinity of the town of Wakefield, an incident took place at 1 a.m.
Saturday morning, July 3 that had an ominous aspect.

A state trooper stopped to offer help to two cars parked on the side of the
road on Interstate 95. Ten men and a lone seventeen-year-old boy came out
of the cars. All were dressed in camouflage clothing and body armor; they
were armed, carrying rifles and pistols. While the leader of the group told the
police that they were traveling to Maine for "training," some of the men ran
away to hide in the woods.

Additional police arrived and the men in the woods returned to their cars
peacefully and were arrested. The search of the cars revealed a large cache
of weapons and ammunition. The leader stated that the group is part of a
national association, Rise of the Moors, Rhode Island based, that does not
recognize the authority of the U.S. government.

The men arrested in Wakefield were from Rhode Island, Michigan, and
New York, heading to Maine for an alleged "training" meet. None had
licenses to carry weapons in Massachusetts.[27]

Did the news of this possibly dangerous event raise alarms of White
supremacists invading our area? The prisoners were detained, refused to
cooperate, refused legal representation, and claimed their innocence of any
crimes. The episode was reported in measured, calm terms by the local newspaper for a few days. No large front-page headlines. No warnings to residents
of the Wakefield area to stay indoors. Why not?

Readers did not learn until the last few lines at the very end of the first news
article that all the accused are African Americans. Now began the excuses.
Mark Pitcavage of the Anti-Defamation League's Center on Extremism, said,

> the sovereign citizen movement is rarely involved in paramilitary activity. "This
> particular group, Rise of the Moors, is actually interested in that so that makes
> them unusual. . . . I find it very ironic . . . that the Moorish sovereign citizen
> movement is so large and active, they actually repeat many theories that were
> actually cooked up, again many years ago, by white supremacists.[28]

Let's parse this presentation of the news. A standoff between Massachusetts
police and a group of armed men who attempt to evade arrest is blithely

portrayed as "no big deal." They're just African American guys traveling to Maine for a weekend in the country. Neither the local press nor the national news made anything of it.

The reader needs less than half a minute to imagine the coverage of this story if the exact same events occurred and the men were White. Seems our local yokels in western Massachusetts have been suitably "trained." They will underplay the importance of even dangerous behavior to be on the correct side of race relations as understood these days.

In recent years, many in the media have eschewed writing about any success stories in racial relations and have instead retreated to the familiar siren call of racial grievances and finger-pointing, in the process exhibiting a form of willful amnesia. It seems only negative items are to be reported, perhaps echoing the brief slogan of the late Marxist Herbert Marcuse, "The Power of Negative Thinking."

Occasionally someone will suggest that racial relations in this country are measurably improved and that this is not an exaggeration. For instance, a recent report by the Manhattan Institute's Eric Kauffman concluded that Whites' approval of Black-White intermarriage rose more than tenfold between 1958 and 1995 and leaped to more than 80 percent by 2013. It would be difficult to cast those numbers in a negative light.

ENDING THIS CONVERSATION

Achieving a racism-free society obviously is a worthwhile goal, but how do we go about attaining it, and how will we know when we have achieved that *desideratum*? There is a fundamental question in play here. What gives anyone the right to presume what is in the heart, mind, or soul of another person based on skin color, much less an entire, diverse group that shares that one trait?

It is a thoroughly irrational assumption, not to mention the height of arrogance and possibly even outright racism itself, to assume we can attribute certain thoughts and attitudes to people we've never met based on race. Better that we judge people by their words and actions, preferably the latter, than by pretending we can read their minds.

The massive efforts required over the decades to push an often-resistant American society to become more equitable and racially inclusive were spearheaded by Black leaders and White leaders as well, who preached the gospel of equality, unity, and a color-blind society that judged people, in the words of Martin Luther King, Jr., not by the color of their skin but by the content of their character. These noble ideals should continue to hold sway in this our multiracial, multiethnic society.

Pursuing the issue of race over the past three years has been broadened, of necessity, by the unusual events in the year 2020. The original considerations on race and anti-racism had to be expanded. This work is a modest attempt to investigate, gather the new ideas of people with important perceptions, to try to understand the enormously difficult times at present, and to imagine the near future.

Writing in the middle of Black History Month 2021 was a time of reflection and serious concern that race relations continue to spiral out of control. Full disclosure: I've watched the entire television series *Roots*, a magnificent portrayal of the arrival of African slaves and their treatment in America. When the work was originally televised in the 1980s, it was used as the basis for English lessons in our classrooms with immigrant children who were mesmerized by the story and its presentation in a series of episodes.

How terribly dismaying to learn today that the largest tech company in the country (in the world?), Amazon, has just committed an act of aggression against a Black American who rose from poverty to become a U.S. Supreme Court Justice. Early in February 2021, Amazon deleted a documentary film, "Created Equal: Clarence Thomas in His Own Words." The film had been televised on PBS and on Amazon in the fall of 2020.

Why was it removed during Black History Month? Amazon refuses to answer that question. The film was well received and had more popularity than other films in the series. By suppressing a film about a Black conservative, Amazon is restricting the public's ability to view the variety of Black positions.

Amazon gives more attention, even during Black History Month, to liberal Blacks and continues to ignore those who are not. Amazon uses its power to promote this effort.[29]

NOTES

1. Mallory Simon, "Over 1,000 Health Professionals Sign a Letter Saying, 'Don't Shut Down Protests Using Coronavirus,'" CNN, June 5, 2020: https://www.cnn.com/2020/06/05/health/health-care-open-letter-protests-coronavirus-trnd/index.html.

2. "Camille Caldera, "San Francisco's Abraham Lincoln High School on Renaming List, but Decision Not Final," *USA Today*, January 28, 2021: https://www.usatoday.com/story/news/factcheck/2020/12/20/fact-check-san-franciscos-abraham-lincoln-hs-name-change-isnt-final/3940580001/.

3. Azi Paybarah, "St. Louis Couple Who Aimed Guns at Protesters Plead Guilty to Misdemeanors," *The New York Times*, June 27, 2021: https://www.nytimes.com/2021/06/17/us/mark-patricia-mccloskey-st-louis-couple-protesters.html.

4. See *1619*, an audio series from the *New York Times*, https://www.nytimes.com/column/1619-project.

5. Glenn C. Loury. "A New American Dilemma." *The New Republic*, 1984: https://www.academia.edu/596293/A_new_American_dilemma.

6. *American Immigrant: My Life in Three Languages*, Transaction Publishers at Rutgers University, Piscataway, New Jersey, 2011.

7. James S. Coleman, "The Concept of Equality in Educational Opportunity," *Harvard Education Review* 38, no. 1, 1968.

8. Glenn C. Loury, "Unspeakable Truths about Racial Inequality in America," Manhattan Institute, February 10, 2021: https://www.manhattan-institute.org/unspeakable-truths-about-racial-inequality-in-america.

9. Rosalie Pedalino Porter, *American Immigrant: My Life in Three Languages* (Piscataway, NJ: Transaction Publishers, 2011).

10. Nada Hassanein, "Young Black Men and Teens Are Killed by Guns 20 Times More Than their White Counterparts, CDC Data Shows," *USA Today*, February 23, 2021: https://www.usatoday.com/story/news/health/2021/02/23/young-black-men-teens-made-up-more-than-third-2019-gun-homicides/4559929001/; The Educational Fund to Stop Gun Violence (EFSGV), "A Public Health Crisis Decades in the Making: A Review of 2019 CDC Gun Mortality Data," February 2021: https://efsgv.org/2019cdcdata/.

11. Loury, "Unspeakable Truths about Racial Inequality in America."

12. Loury, "Unspeakable Truths about Racial Inequality in America."

13. Sarah Metcalf, "Whose Streets? Our Children's Streets," *Daily Hampshire Gazette*, September 29, 2021.

14. Weiss, "Wrongthink on Race with Glenn Loury."

15. "The Weekend Interview with Shelby Steele: How Equality Lost to Equity," Tunku Varadarajan, Wall Street Journal, February 13, 2021.

16. Charles Lipson, "Equity Is a Mandate to Discriminate," *The Wall Street Journal*, March 4, 2021: https://www.wsj.com/articles/equity-is-a-mandate-to-discriminate-11614901276.

17. Lipson, "Equity Is a Mandate to Discriminate."

18. Princeton's Office of Communication, "An Update and Overview of Princeton University's Ongoing Efforts to Combat Systemic Racism," September 2, 2020: https://www.princeton.edu/news/2020/09/02/update-and-overview-princeton-universitys-ongoing-efforts-combat-systemic-racism.

19. "Jacquelyn Voghel, "Amherst College Takes Lead in Condemning Education Department Targeting Princeton," *Daily Hampshire Gazette*, September 29, 2020: https://www.gazettenet.com/Princeton-hg-093020-36513821.

20. Steve Pfarrer, "Amherst College Bicentennial. Evolving: Early men's Religious School Turned to Liberal Arts and Science, and It's Been Shedding a Reputation for Privilege with a Focus on Diversity," *Daily Hampshire Gazette*, September 21, 2021.

21. Mike Powell, "Inside a Battle over Race, Class and Power at Smith College," *The New York Times*, February 24, 2021: https://www.nytimes.com/2021/02/24/us/smith-college-race.html.

22. Robert L. Woodson et al., "1776 Unites Open Letter to Smith College," March 22, 2021: https://1776unites.com/essays/1776-unites-open-letter-to-smith-college/.

23. Bret Stephens, "Smith College and the Failing Liberal Bargain," *The New York Times*, March 1, 2021: https://www.nytimes.com/2021/03/01/opinion/smith-college -race-class.html.

24. Chelsea Kline, "White People, We Have Bad Breath," *Daily Hampshire Gazette*, May 3, 2021: https://www.gazettenet.com/Columnist-Chelsea-Kline-40229843.

25. Andrea Ayvazian, "Are We an Enclave of 'Nice Racists'"? *Daily Hampshire Gazette*, September 18, 2021: https://www.gazettenet.com/Guest-columnist-Andrea -Ayvazian-42481274.

26. Robin DiAngelo, *Nice Racism: How Progressive White People Perpuate Racial Harm* (New York: Penguin Random House, 2021).

27. "Mass. Police: Suspects in Armed Highway Standoff Members of Self-Styled 'Moorish' Militia," *Daily Hampshire Gazette*, July 5, 2021: https://www.gazettenet .com/Massachusetts-police-ID-suspects-in-armed-highway-standoff-41295480.

28. "Mass. Police: Suspects in Armed Highway Standoff."

29. Jason L. Riley, "Why Did Amazon Cancel Justice Thomas?," *The Wall Street Journal*, March 2, 2021: https://www.wsj.com/articles/why-did-amazon-cancel -justice-thomas-11614727562.

Critical Race Theory

How to Destroy the U.S. by Educational Indoctrination

On his first day in office, January 20, 2021, President Joseph Biden rescinded former President Trump's Executive Order 13950 prohibiting Critical race theory (CRT) training for federal agencies and federal contractors. President Biden followed this order on January 25, 2021, with Executive Order 14035 titled "Diversity, Equity, Inclusion, and Accessibility in the Federal Workforce," The executive order that President Trump had signed on September 22, 2020, was titled "Combating Racial and Sex Stereotyping."[1]

The subject of these two executive actions, by two presidents, raises the antennas of serious concern on an issue not widely known among the general population. What was deemed so perilous in the Trump order that an incoming president would make it a significant, first-day-in-office priority?

In the past decade, critical race theory, like the new anti-racism movement and Black Lives Matter, has been percolating along, trickling down, and slowly gaining public attention. Like other progressive movements, these ideologies lived mostly on college campuses but were beginning to penetrate and affect the worlds of public education, corporations, and government bureaucracies. Critical race theory is one offshoot of the critical legal studies movement that started in the countries' law schools in the late 1970s and the radical feminism movement of the same period.

CRITICAL LEGAL THEORY: THE PROGENITOR OF CRITICAL RACE THEORY

Critical legal theory, incubated in law schools, is traced for its first public announcement at a conference at the University of Wisconsin/Madison in

1977. Its basic theory proposes that the law is intertwined with social issues and has social biases. U.S. law favors the historically privileged and disadvantages the historically underprivileged. It is a means for oppression. Critical legal theory (CLT) plans to overturn modern societies by using this tool—critical legal studies.

Critical legal theory is Marxist influenced and advances the radical theories of the usual suspects, for example, Foucault, Freire, Gramschi, and others. The umbrella beliefs of critical legal theory generated spinoffs or subgroups such as feminist legal theory (the role of gender and the law), critical race theory (the role of race and the law), and postmodernism (the role of social issues in literature and the law).[2]

CRITICAL RACE THEORY: WHAT IT IS AND HOW IT DEFINES ITS GOALS

Critical race theory merits serious investigation, explanation, and a reasoned judgment of its benefits or disadvantages on the areas in American public life that it is more and more affecting. The route taken in this essay is to define the ideology from opposing viewpoints, assess its effects in different arenas, and come to some conclusions on its value. In just the time since the beginning of the COVID-19 pandemic, the topic has become highly visible in the public domain and initiated the beginnings of a strong push back from some of the people in its crosshairs.

On hearing the title alone, one might dismiss it as a bit of academic sophistry, far removed from normal, everyday life. That would be a mistake of large proportions. Richard Delgado and Jean Stefancic, the authors of *Critical Race Theory: An Introduction*, provide a comprehensive view of the subject. The authors question the very basics of a liberal society, discounting such accepted democratic norms as equality, scientific rationalism, and constitutional laws.

Delgado and Stefancic hold strong beliefs in the fundamental racism of this country (as does the entire anti-racism movement and Black Lives Matter) and dismiss out of hand the accomplishments of the past half dozen decades. They do not acknowledge, much less credit, the civil rights movement from the 1960s on, or the laws passed or rulings from the courts to bring progress to Blacks and improve racial relations across the country. They deny any real progress.

In their views, our laws may have changed, but the continued existence of White privilege has not. In order to overcome that stasis, change must come, not by incremental steps like affirmative action, but by a substantial overthrow of the country as we know it—that is, real revolutionary change.

Derrick Bell may be the most highly qualified Black legal scholar to advance critical race theory. He is considered the founder, the godfather of the genre. Bell who was the first Black to earn tenure at Harvard Law School, published legal works as well as fiction. In his 1992 book of essays, *Faces at the Bottom of the Well: The Permanence of Racism,* Bell reveals a profoundly negative view of race in our country, a view that has influenced activists of present times, such as Ta-Nehisi Coates and Michelle Alexander: "In the conclusion to *Faces,* Bell argues that the struggle for racial equality is worthwhile even though it will never succeed . . . Bell demands recognition of the futility of action while insisting that action must be taken."[3]

At a Harvard Law School conference in 1991, a political scientist whose work focuses on race and inequality reacted with surprise to Profess Bell's comments: "I heard the late esteemed legal theorist Derrick Bell declare on a panel that blacks had made no progress since 1865. I was startled, not least because of Bell's own life, as well as the fact that Harvard's black law students' organization put on the conference, so emphatically belied his claim."[4]

Critical race theory's disavowal of the Reverend Martin Luther King's beliefs is total. King's dream of a color-blind society that brought our nation's people together is passe. The aims of the new constellation of activists in the critical race theory camp is vindicative, divisive, and calls for reparations for past injustices. There is a whiff here of visiting the sins of past generations on our present people, guilt for the injustices committed by people who may or may not have been our ancestors given the enormous variety of ethnic immigrants over the past four hundred years.

To begin to overcome racism, according to our friends on the left, will necessarily be a long row to hoe, and will require color-conscious efforts, that is, anti-White discrimination. And the way to bring this about is through education, that is, re-education in the style of the old Soviet camps and gulags. Mandated training in every area of our culture, from kindergarten through graduate school, in the workplace, in the military, in government.

The design of this essay is to start with effects and outcomes of critical race theory efforts in the free market workplace, in academia, as experienced in the Chinese American community, and finally, in the most sensitive and potentially most damaging place of all—K–12 public education.

AN EVALUATION OF DIVERSITY
TRAINING IN THE WORKPLACE

As mentioned in the introduction to this essay, President Biden's promise in his inaugural address was to do his all to unite the nation. His executive order to reimpose diversity training programs was to further this goal. Average people will commend efforts that in fact reduce bias, racism, and sexism in this country and will appreciate training programs that demonstrate some improvements.

Concentrating the president's aim on programs that are so widely adopted of late that they are a multi-billion-dollar industry, there are legitimate questions to be raised as to their effectiveness. Two obvious reasons for investing in such programs may be (1) the progressive insistence that we are a country mired in all kinds of racism that must be overcome, and (2) the notion that inequities still exist among different racial groups in education and economic achievements, in attaining a decent standard of living.

Two social scientists, Helen Hemphill and Ray Haines, completed a five-year study, conducting interviews with five hundred managers and directors as well as discussions with one hundred diversity consultants and trainers. They studied the research on diversity training in the workplace. Of their eleven conclusions that they declared to be "overwhelming in their consistency," the major conclusions are listed here:

- participants in these workshops found them to be divisive, disturbing, and counterproductive;
- diversity trainers were often inexperienced and ineffective;
- White males were stereotyped and blamed; and
- distrust between men and women increased.[5]

A recent report by Columbia University professor Musa al-Gharbi, cited in the aforementioned article, summarizes the research to date and concludes that "most diversity training divides more than it unites, reinforces stereotypes and worsens intergroup relations, while failing to increase diversity in leadership or enhance productivity."[6]

It is not unreasonable to ask why these programs have grown so large and popular and costly when there is so little known of any successful outcomes. On reflection, there are several commonsense answers. People of good will want our society to overcome racism and will readily welcome programs that root out this scourge and make this improvement happen, an ethical and moral imperative.

There is always the profit motive to consider, and diversity training is a multi-billion-dollar industry for consulting companies doing the training and for the universities training the trainers. There is a subtle but real fear for business leaders and government bureaucrats. Diversity training is publicly acknowledged to be essential and so an investment is made. Human resources departments fell in love with this new fad and have given themselves an immodest cover for virtue signaling.

If, after the investment of company time and money, there is no visible or clear benefit from this training, it might still be a dangerous folly for business firms or government agencies to cancel further programs of this sort. The risk of being publicly shamed and derided would surely be bad for business. In our obsessive era of "cancel culture," who could dare take such a risk?

LOCKHEED, DISNEY, AMERICAN EXPRESS, AND WALMART

A few examples will establish that diversity training workshops are flourishing. The first two examples are brief, while the American Express and Walmart training programs merit much broader attention.

At the Lockheed Corporation, workshop sessions forced White men to take part, for three days, in training sessions that would deconstruct their "white male culture" and make them atone for their "white male privilege."

The Disney Corporation provided a program that taught its workers about America's racist structure and urged them to "think carefully about whether or not your wealth, income, treatment by the criminal justice system, employment, access to housing, political power, and education might be different if you were of a different race."[7]

AMERICAN EXPRESS CORPORATION STEPS FORWARD

Just since the killing of George Floyd in 2020, the American Express Corporation (AmEx) has created a comprehensive training program to teach employees to analyze their individual standing and to know that the corporation that employs them and capitalism itself are racist. The training asks employees to deconstruct their racial and sexual identities and judge themselves on their levels of "privilege."

An employee whistleblower secretly provided critical race theory critic Christopher F. Rufo with extensive material on the American Express program and its negative view not only of itself as a corporation but of our entire national culture. An introductory session imposes on the employees the obligation to analyze themselves and enter the information on an official worksheet for the company: sex, age, gender identity, and disability.

Each employee uses this "map" to determine whether they have "privilege" or belong to a group that is undervalued in our society. The assumption is that straight White males are at one end of the oppressor scale, and racial and sexual minorities and women are in the oppressed position.

An essential lesson for office behavior imposes a rule that the privileged must always defer to Black, female, and LGBTQ employees, always allowing them to speak first. Also, the privileged must self-censor the words or phrases used in office conversations. How much more intrusive into people's personal lives can office rules get? Can such restrictions on staff relations in the office workday possibly have beneficial effects?

A large conference was planned by AmEx, for an extended discussion of the responsibilities of the corporation. The invited speaker, Professor Elijah Muhammad, was brought forward to lecture the company on racism in corporate America. His statement of accusation was quite clear, "[Y]ou are complicit in giving privileges in one community against the other, under the pretext that we live in a meritocratic system where the market judges everyone the same."

The good professor's advice was that AmEx should charge Black customers less than others for services, and that the company could do good by adopting business practices that don't maximize profit. This would appear to be unrealistic advice for a service business.

The final insult to all their employees is passing on the advice of the diversity trainers to recommend certain readings on these topics: articles that demonstrate that white children become racist before they can speak; articles that ask employees to dedicate themselves to a lifelong task of fighting racism; and pieces that persuade employees to lobby Congress to pass race-based reparations legislation.

Two thoughts to conclude this scurrilous account of corporate leadership's weakness of brain power and/or backbone. Whistleblowers allege that AmEx is creating an internal climate of fear and division, and the evidence here suggests it may be true. The other point to ponder is the obvious illegality of disseminating training materials that violate the prohibitions in the Civil Rights Act against racial stereotyping and scapegoating in the workplace.[8]

On the notion that Whites must be prepared to spend their whole lives working to rid themselves of the racism lodged in their DNA, is it possible that Whites may be able, by their study and good works, to overcome racism? That would be an inspiring goal to aim for, but there is no existing measure or standard to prove it. The Greeks had a concept for this, the myth of Sisyphus, the Sisyphean, never-ending, pushing a stone up a steep mountain and failing to reach the summit. A harsher judgment would be to label it fraudulent, utopian mythmaking.

Coming back to earth from the cosmic zone, a mundane, everyday question to pose to the managers at AmEx is to ask if they have yet estimated how many ordinary Americans would, on reading this story, cancel their AmEx cards?

WALMART INC. VS. WHITENESS:
SEGREGATION AND BRAINWASHING

Since 2018, Walmart Inc. has provided a training program for employees that hews to the basic ideas of critical race theory, with these themes: the United States is a "white supremacy system," and Walmart's White workers must be taught that they are guilty of "white supremacy thinking," that they have internalized a condition of "racial superiority," while non-Whites are afflicted with "internalized racial inferiority." The agency providing this training is the Racial Equity Institute of Greensboro, North Carolina.[9]

The training curriculum has already enrolled over a thousand employees. The training is mandatory for executives, and it is recommended for hourly wage workers in the Walmart stores. The opening salvo in the training session is that White Europeans developed the United States as a way of "maintaining white skin access to power and privilege."[10] Apparently it is a verifiable fact to the trainers teaching Walmart classes that all those explorers from Genoa, Spain, Portugal, and England had one mind set: take over new lands only to preserve the power of Whites.

The next lesson is to dismiss any government program that is race neutral—that's not good enough to heal the lack of opportunity that people of color have suffered these past four hundred years in the United States. The trainers claim that President Obama's stimulus legislation in 2009 benefited White people more than Blacks. The conclusion is that economic programs must be designed specifically for people of color and leave Whites out of it if a balance of opportunity is to be achieved.

Like other programs of this type, it is highly recommended that "discussions about racist conditioning should be conducted in racially segregated 'affinity groups' because people of color and white people have their own work to do in understanding and addressing racism."[11] It may seem deeply counterproductive to most Americans with any knowledge of the years of effort expended to rid our country of segregation. Does it make sense that in this millennium we would approve of placing people in segregated groups to learn better lessons about racism?

The most shocking and unprecedented idea in the Walmart training program is that Whites have been diagnosed with a psychological condition that can be treated through "white anti-racism development." The notion that an entire cohort of people can be classified as mentally unstable due to their skin color and in need of treatment by the ministrations of the Racial Equity Institute defies logic. Whites, it is said, will be cured once they accept their guilt and shame, acknowledge their racism, and try to make themselves over with a new anti-racist identity.

The Walmart corporation employs the highest number of people of any corporation in the world. It is a matter of record that their executives are among the most highly paid people on earth. There is a suspicion that these business leaders are gaining honor and admiration for mounting such a worthy cause as anti-racism training, demonstrating their virtue.

For the hourly wage employees who earn between $25,000 and $30,000 a year, do they need to sit in classes where they are humiliated for their "white privilege"? Somehow this scene does not seem equitable or of much value for the hourly wage earners.[12]

A SPECIAL CASE: CRITICAL RACE THEORY AND ASIAN-AMERICANS IN HIGHER EDUCATION

The Chinese American Citizens Alliance Greater New York (CACAGNY) posted an attack titled "CACAGNY Denounces Critical Race Theory as Hateful Fraud" on February 23, 2021. Their basic claim is that critical race theory, contrary to its representation by the media, academia, and progressives as an anti-racism model for equity and inclusion is exactly the opposite: "From its very roots, CRT is racist, repressive, discriminatory and divisive."

These are strong accusations that deserve attention. The negative effects of critical race theory on Americans of Chinese descent are real and the CACAGNY provides its views on the issue, with some ideas for pushing back against it.

CACAGNY is not alone in contending that the best-known figures behind critical race theory ideology are the radical progressives taught in college courses for decades: Marx, Lenin, Marcuse, Foucault, and Freire, with race struggle now replacing class struggle. In the view of CACAGNY, these are a few of the critical race theory principles to which they strongly object:

- You are not a person, you are only your race, and will be judged only by your race.
- Only social justice matters; justice does not. To achieve equal outcomes, forget equal rights.
- All Blacks are oppressed; all Whites are oppressors. Everyone and everything White is complicit.
- To reduce Whites' implicit bias, Whites must self-criticize, confess to privilege, and apologize to the oppressed race.
- CRT suppresses dissent with cancel culture: publications withdrawn, college admissions rescinded, jobs terminated.[13]

The main thrust of the complaint against these ideas is to describe the effect they have on the Chinese descent community in the United States. This impact is mainly in the area of education. It is a widely known fact that in recent years complaints about too many Asians in the most selective schools are routine.

In the earlier years of the civil rights movement, Asians were grouped with "people of color" and were deemed oppressed people. Since this group began to overcome discrimination and gained upward mobility, they have now been labeled *White by adjacency.*

The lawsuit brought against Harvard University for its "multiple-criteria holistic admission" criteria for student admissions will be heard by the U.S. Supreme Court in the 2022–2023 session. The "holistic" ruse will finally be judged a flimsy excuse to deny admissions on merit and favor racial preferences. The false criteria favoring "holistic" admissions has the unintended effect of lowering academic standards. Clearly, this approach is aimed at getting rid of too many Asians in elite schools, which may be seen as today's Chinese Exclusion Act, a hate crime against Asians.

An interesting point is made by CACAGNY regarding current immigration. It is claimed that critical race theory may bump up against the tide of new immigrants and their values. Immigrants, including Blacks from West Africa and the Caribbean, are making real progress as they come to the United States to work hard and to educate their children. They believe in the American dream and in the guarantee of equal rights. How will CRT handle such idolatry in our White racist country?

CACAGNY advises parents of school children to recognize critical race theory in their children's curriculum and "call it out—resist it." They urge parents to speak with their children and un-doctrinate them at home from the constant focus on race and anti-racism.

On the political and legal front, this organization is working to get representatives elected in New York who represent their views and are filing several lawsuits against compelled speech and hostile work environments created by critical race theory. Their ambitions are commendable.

HIGHER EDUCATION AND THE *NEW YORK TIMES* 1619 PROJECT

In the 1950s, academia was firmly under the control of conservative scholars and the political power of Cold War extremists. The world of higher education has changed dramatically in the past few decades. The former minority of left-leaning professors has grown to constitute the overwhelming majority of faculty and administrators.

Most glaringly out of balance is the ratio of liberal to conservative faculty. In his new book, *A Time to Build: From Family and Community to Congress and the Campus, How Recommitting to Our Institutions Can Revive the American Dream*, Yuval Levin declares the situation to be this: "[T]the university is now a monoculture, virtually without debate. In the humanities and social sciences, liberals and those who lean left outweigh those who are moderate or conservative by about fifty to one."[14]

Time to introduce a local event demonstrating that in the case where two priorities clash, one may gain prime place. Following the 1960s decade of chaos on college campuses, higher education was intensely focused on generating greater diversity in student enrollment and in the faculty. Professor Ralph Beals, head of the economics department at Amherst College, recruited an exceptionally qualified economist, Thomas Sowell, an African American. What a coup for this elite college that almost always ranks first or second in the country in lists of comparable schools.

Professor Beals had sufficient evidence, at the end of Sowell's year of lecturing, to know that they had a valuable African American candidate, admired by colleagues and students alike. He recommended to the administration that Sowell be offered a tenure-track appointment. Beals was deeply disappointed when his nomination of Sowell was not approved. How could the college not want to have such a prominent African American on its faculty? The reason was spelled out to him: Sowell is a conservative. Even at a time of serious diversity efforts, politics trumped race.[15]

THE HYPER-INDULGENCE OF STUDENTS

Well-documented on campus and in the mainstream press in recent years are the impositions of speech codes, microaggression rules, safe spaces, trigger warnings, and puritanical rules on social conduct. These new restrictions are promoted to protect every student, that is everyone but Whites, from ever feeling a moment of doubt or hurt, or ever reading about or hearing an idea that may disturb a person's self-pride.

Higher education looks more and more like an all-encompassing nanny state, not the place to open minds to intellectual diversity. At the same time, the proportion of male to female enrollments in colleges and universities has reversed. In 2022 women make up 60 percent of all college students to 40 percent for men (percentages are rounded). This radical change may be attributable to several causes, a large factor being excessive increases in tuition costs making four-year college prohibitive.

It may also be a factor of the treatment of men on campus, the rise in anti-male animus is openly expressed in classrooms and in social situations.

The increase in racial and ethnic studies programs plays a part as too often these programs concentrate on demonizing and demoralizing white males.

In earlier generations, faculty, students, and even college presidents protested the Vietnam War, agitated in favor of civil rights for African Americans and other worthwhile causes. The consensus in academia was that these projects merited the public protests of intelligent Americans. Over time, these laudable protests achieved their goals.

The ill-conceived U.S. involvement in Vietnam ended in 1975, and civil rights and government investments in minority communities were pursued. Not perfection, as there will always be disruptive events to overcome, but times were relatively placid until 9/11 and the start of our nation's involvement in Afghanistan and surroundings to combat anti-American terrorism. The next flash points are the chaos of the 2020 election and its aftermath, the dual catastrophes of the shutdown of the world due to the COVID-19 pandemic and the outbursts in our country after the death of George Floyd.

A few years ago, the politically correct thinkers on campus pronounced a new ideology, and social justice emerged to eradicate the sins of the fathers (i.e., the founders of our country and the Constitution they created and signed in 1776). The political movement to rewrite American history, the 1619 Project, found fertile ground in the aggrieved young students seeking a cause, and became the impetus for the doctrines of the new anti-racism of Black leaders leaning far on the left.

DISDAINING OUR ANCIENT EUROCENTRIC HISTORY

"We can never cut ourselves off from antiquity unless we intend to revert to barbarism. The barbarian and the creature of exclusively modern civilization both live without history."—Jacob Burckhardt[16]

It has long been an accepted understanding in academia that some Eurocentric disciplines have outlived their usefulness in the modern world, that is, the new millennium. The study of Greek and Roman civilizations may be beneath contempt, by our new standards, considered to be irremediably stuck in racist ideals.

In the desire to cleanse all sins of the past, where shall we draw the line in negating the study of our common historical backgrounds? This is too large a question for this book, but it is worth noting that the Greco-Roman period, what we call "The Classics," is currently a target of the anti-racist crowd. Oddly enough it appears that some of the most revered scholars of the classics are leading the charge to eliminate their discipline. The other oddity worth noting, on the other hand, is that a few Black scholars are defending the importance of studying the classics.

Two professors long respected as Stanford University scholars of the classics are quoted recently with highly negative views. Professor Ian Morris states, "Classics is a Euro-American foundational myth. Do we really want that sort of thing?" While his colleague, Walter Scheidel agrees: "I don't think it should exist as an academic field."[17] Those are pretty extreme views by academics who have been very well paid, have risen to the top of their field, and now suddenly consign it to extinction.

The *New York Times* featured a Princeton professor who may be the most extreme and, therefore, the most popular proponent of this idea. Dan-el Padilla Peralta of the Princeton University classics department rests his reputation now on weeding out the racism of Whites that has come down to us from the old racism of the ancient world. Are his ideas historically documented? Some say that is not true.

And if we want to savor a truly thrilling idea from this associate professor of classics at Princeton, Professor Padilla spoke these words in a video at the freshman orientation, September 2021:

> I envision a free speech and an intellectual discourse that is flexed to one specific aim, the promotion of social justice . . . to provide effective mentoring to our students, not to indoctrinating them to the view that this is "the best damn place of all," but in order to supply them with the tools with which they can tear down this place and make it a better one.[18]

The notion of a Princeton professor professing to teach students ways to "tear down the place" has a bitter memory from the Vietnam War era when a U.S. Army officer was asked why he had his troops destroy a whole village, and his famous quote was "We had to destroy it to save it."

Were the Greeks and Romans racists? Victor Davis Hanson provides substantial proofs to the contrary: "Whiteness itself was a concept completely unknown to the Greeks and Romans. No such word exists in the classical vocabularies of the ancient world. . . . 'Nordic' phenotypes were usually in reference to tribal peoples of more remote and colder climates, pre-civilized clans such as the Gauls, Germans or Thracians."[19]

Padilla of Princeton may be demonstrating the highest virtue signaling possible in his willingness to sacrifice his own professional career rather than continue teaching a harmful subject. Following in his wake, though, there may be the unintended destruction of the jobs of thousands of high school Latin teachers who are probably not yet in the "woke" camp.

In April 2021, two prominent scholars published their defense of the classics in an article in the *Washington Post*. Black philosophy professor

Cornel West and critical legal theory founder Jeremy Tate authored "Howard University's Removal of Classics Is a Spiritual Catastrophe." They deplore the fact that the classics are not much supported in academia, especially in recent times. But their greatest dismay is over the historically Black institution, Howard University, canceling its classics department: "Engaging with the classics and with our civilizational heritage is the means to finding our true voice. It is how we become our full selves, spiritually free and morally great . . . the classics approach is united to the Black experience."[20]

It may be that West and Tate were influenced in their defense of the classics by the work of Frank M. Snowden, an African American scholar of high reputation at Howard University. His publications over thirty years focused research on the art and literature of the ancient world and racial attitudes they revealed. Snowden concluded that "Greeks and Romans were mostly oblivious to modern notions of racial prejudice. . . . [C]lassical references to black people were often favorable, while northern European 'whites' were usually assumed to be savage and tribal."[21]

HISTORICAL REVISIONISM IN THE U.S.: THE *NEW YORK TIMES* 1619 PROJECT

In August 2019, a special issue of the *New York Times* Sunday magazine presented a long journalistic piece by Nikole Hannah-Jones of the University of North Carolina. The 1619 Project is not simply an essay but was introduced as a multi-platform campaign launched by the *New York Times* and the Pulitzer Center for Crisis Journalism, a powerful collaborative effort. Hannah-Jones's central ideas that overturn traditional American history are controversial and summarized here:

1. The origin of America's entire history and character are based on the arrival of slaves in Virginia in 1619.
2. The War of Independence was fought to stop the British from outlawing slavery.
3. American capitalism was created and still operates on relations rooted in plantation slavery.
4. Africans were alone and had no allies in their fight for civil and human rights.
5. Abraham Lincoln was a racist who worked to keep the races separate and maintain the oppression of Africans Americans.[22]

Does journalist Hannah-Jones prove her historical claims with sufficient factual data? Apparently not. The 1619 theory has been challenged by such noted historians as Gordon Wood and James McPherson for its lack of evidence to substantiate such a radically different picture of the beginnings of American history.

THE 1619 PROJECT ATTRACTS SEVERE CRITICISM

One of the most vocal and publicly prominent Black leaders opposing the 1619 portrayal of the founding of our country is business leader Robert L. Woodson, Sr. His Woodson Center provides support for local initiatives in poor Black neighborhoods mired in gang activity, failing schools, and lack of opportunity. His central belief is that helping Blacks help themselves is far more effective than calling for more government intrusions.[23]

Mr. Woodson is passionate in his criticism of the 1619 Project for dismissing facts in favor of creating new fictions of our early history. He convened a conference of Black scholars and activists—1776 Unites—to confront the 1619 rhetoric. A collection of essays from that meeting is in Mr. Woodson's new book published in May 2021, *Red, White and Black: Rescuing American History from Revisionists and Race Hustlers.* In the book's introduction, he writes that he wants to "debunk the myth that present-day problems are related to our past . . . specifically, debunking the myth that slavery is the source of present-day disparities and injustice."[24]

Were it only a scholarly debate among historians, conducted in scholarly articles of interest only to their academic colleagues, it would just be a benign exercise. But it has broadened into an educational industry spreading its curriculum materials, at no cost, in K–12 public schools across the country.

Peter Wood in his 2020 book, *1620: A Critical Response to the 1619 Project*, claims the original event of 1619 was the arrival of a group of Africans who had been captured at sea by pirates and landed on the Virginia coast where they were traded to the colonists in exchange for food. True they were kept as indentured servants but not as slaves, as slavery from Europe did not arrive for several decades.

Wood subscribes to the alternate view that the Mayflower Compact, the agreement between the Pilgrims arriving on the New England coast and the colonists in Northern Virginia, is the foundational document of our country. It was the historical contract pledging the early settlers to devote themselves to the pursuit of the common good under law. Wood is concerned about the effect of 1619 on the young who are being taught a new and factually unsupported history of their country. As well, he deplores Hannah-Jones statements denying that facts are central to the study of history.[25]

Professor Wood refutes the common misconception that slavery was introduced to the Western Hemisphere after the arrival of Christopher Columbus at the end of the fifteenth century. In fact, evidence points to the existence of slavery in this part of the world long before that: "It was an institution familiar to many native societies in both North and South America. These populations had been enslaving one another, as far as we can tell, from time immemorial . . .. The year 1492 changed the world but not by introducing slavery to the Americas. Slavery was already here."[26]

An amusing aside on the *New York Times*' fact checking is provided by a colleague of Hannah-Jones who was enlisted to check some facts in the 1619 Project. Leslie Harris, a professor of history at Northwestern University, specializes in African American life and slavery before the Civil War. An editor at the *New York Times* wrote to ask her to verify this statement from the Hannah-Jones work:

> One critical reason that the colonists declared their independence from the British was because they wanted to protect the institution of slavery, which had produced tremendous wealth. At the time there were growing calls to abolish slavery throughout the British Empire, which would have badly damaged the economies of the colonies in both north and south.

Professor Harris's response emphatically denied that this statement was a historical fact. "Although slavery was certainly an issue in the American Revolution, the protection of slavery was not one of the main reasons the 13 Colonies went to war."[27]

NIKOLE HANNAH-JONES, SUPERSTAR

Hannah-Jones emerges as a successful journalist, with a prestigious MacArthur genius grant. She is being honored for her 1619 publication with a Pulitzer Prize in 2021. It does seem a bit odd that the cosponsor of the 1619 Project, the Pulitzer Center for Crisis Journalism, would then confer the Pulitzer Prize on this work that they themselves brought into the world.

Professor Hannah-Jones has been on the faculty of the Hussman School of Journalism and Media at the University of North Carolina since 2015. In 2021 she was offered a five-year contract at the university, which she declined, opting instead to be granted tenure. In June 2021, she was nominated to the board of trustees for tenure. It was not an easy sell.

Opposition to the tenure was voiced most urgently by a large donor to the university for whom the journalism center is named, Walter Sussman. He took exception to Hannah-Jones dismissal of objectivity in journalism and was concerned at the widespread accusations of prominent historians that the 1619 Project was a distortion of historical records. Mr. Sussman was convinced that the project did not adhere to his ideas of the core values for journalism of integrity, impartiality, pursuit of truth, and the separation of news from public opinion.

Mr. Sussman's objections did not prevail. After a closed three-hour meeting of the board of trustees, the majority voted to confer tenure on Hannah-Jones.[28]

TURNING TO THE EFFECTS OF CRITICAL RACE THEORY ON K–12 PUBLIC EDUCATION

Our nation's public schools educating children in grades kindergarten through grade 12 are not exemplary models of success, compared with the achievements in other developed countries. Since the 1970s the demand for greater funding to improve public education has been generally pursued with vigor and good results. *A Nation at Risk* set the early tone.

Greater annual funding from state and federal sources is a matter of record. Investments in all areas—school construction, curriculum development, testing, increasing teacher salaries, programs for special populations, integration—have been well funded, evaluated, and when necessary, revised and improved. We should expect to see better outcomes in student achievement, especially for minority students from families of poverty who need extra help the most.

President Jimmy Carter's administration created the new Department of Education to support state education efforts and gather data on public education results, a department that has grown over the years. It is important to look at some data of recent vintage on U.S. students' performance on basic subjects essential to all learning, reading and math. The National Assessment of Educational Progress (NAEP), a national, annual test for fourth and eighth graders across the country reported the following in 2019:

- high school seniors' performance on the reading test recorded a seven-point drop;
- a majority of fourth and eighth graders cannot do grade level work in reading or math;
- math scores for high school students show no improvement in a decade; and
- 82 percent of high school students graduated on time, but only a third of them are academically prepared for college coursework in reading and math.[29]

The National Assessment of Educational Progress is traditionally referred to as "the nation's report card" and is respected as a valid measure for comparing student achievement across the country. American students do not fare well when compared with students in other developed countries, in spite of our higher level of spending on public education. On a recent international survey of thirty-four countries, "American high school students ranked in the middle of the nations in their reading, math and science, while 25 of the nations surveyed had higher graduation rates than the U.S."[30]

Reports of student performance since the COVID-19 pandemic are not yet reliably available, but it is fair to surmise that the learning loss has been severe. Will school districts think outside the box and plan extra programs to make up for the lost time, perhaps with extra hours in the school day, summer classes, or after-school tutoring?

It is a common fact, but our readers must be reminded, that the United States has the shortest school day and school year in the developed world. Our 180-day school year and six-hour school day compares very unfavorably with most countries 220 school days and more hours in the school day. It is an educational truism that the more time spent on studying a subject, the better it will be learned, providing all factors other than time are equal (i.e., trained teachers, available textbooks and materials, etc.).

What help can it possibly be for students to be burdened with a new emphasis in their school experience, not enrichment of reading, writing, math, or science, but the imposition of the 1619 Project in their history classes? The goal of 1619 is to focus children on race, away from traditional facts of the early founding years, and to inculcate the disputed facts prescribed by critical race theory.

In the upscale town of Wellesley, Massachusetts, we have an example of an unusual way that this district implemented the new ideas of dividing themselves to promote equity, the implied good outcome of critical race theory. Documents obtained by the Judicial Watch organization under the Massachusetts Public Records Law reveal that the school district is segregating students and teachers into "affinity" groups, with five distinct segregated spaces.

The program has been in place from September 1, 2020, to May 17, 2021. The stated goal of this effort is to amplify student voices for students with a shared identity. This can hardly be disguised as anything but a plan that has deliberately promoted the dividing of staff and students by skin color or ethnicity or some category of oppression, into "healing spaces"—whatever that term may mean. The ACLU should certainly be investigating this Wellesley program.[31]

According to the Claremont Institute, more than 3,500 classrooms across America are including 1619 lesson plans in their history curriculum, including school districts in Chicago, Illinois; Newark, New Jersey; Buffalo, New York; and Washington, DC.[32] This is an accomplishment of enormous proportions, considering that the 1619 Project was only published in 2019. Two of the most powerful players in this drama, using their bully pulpit to promote 1619 in the schools, are the teachers' unions, the National Education Association (NEA), and the American Federation of Teachers (AFT).

In July 2021 at their annual meeting, the National Education Association adopted a proposal stating that "it is reasonable and appropriate for curriculum to be informed by academic frameworks for understanding and interpreting the impact of the past on current society, including critical race theory."[33]

The organization pledged to "fight back against anti-CRT rhetoric . . . and issue a study that critiques empire, white supremacy, anti-Blackness, anti-Indigeneity, racism, patriarchy, cisheteropatriarchy, capitalism, ableism, anthropocentrism, and other forms of power and oppression at the intersections of our society."[34]

Just reading the list of the evils that the National Education Association highlights for opposition in our schools will overwhelm any average, moderately educated adult. The idea that teaching young children such topics to mold their attitudes as they grow up is not only absurd but harmful and clearly age inappropriate.

Not to be outdone, the American Federation of Teachers signs to the ideas of Ibram X. Kendi whose notoriety rests on his advocacy for racial discrimination against Whites. Mr. Kendi was a speaker at the AFT annual meeting in July 2021, and the union leaders stated that "they will donate copies of Mr. Kendi's writings to schools, AFT members, educators, and youth mentors."[35]

The stand taken by the American Federation of Teachers is no less alarming than that of the National Education Association, for it, too, seems to privilege indoctrination, divisions, and political attitudes over actual subject matter learning. No sign here of any interest in making serious efforts to improve school children's performance in reading, math, and science.

PARENTS OF SCHOOL CHILDREN
BEGIN TO PUSH BACK

It was inevitable that in the year 2020 with the lockdown of parents and children, to work and study in the home for months at a time, parents would be more closely attuned to just what the children were being taught. As the first stories about critical race theory began to appear in the media, the push back began in cities and towns across the country from New York to San Francisco.

The expressions of protest are coming from across racial groups, and it appears to be a non-partisan movement. Among the explosion of protests that have erupted, a few examples paint the general outlines of the story.

Tatiana Ibraham protested to the Carmel School Board in Putnam County, New York, that teachers and administrators were promoting "communist values," saying, "Stop indoctrinating our children. Stop teaching our children to hate the police. Stop teaching our children that if they don't agree with the LGBT community they're homophobic. . . . You have no idea of each child's life," and she mentioned that she is a Christian and her daughter is a Muslim.[36]

Quisha King, a mother in Duval County, Florida, expressed equal outrage: "Telling my child or any child that they are in a permanent oppressed status in America because they are black is racist—and saying that white people are automatically above me, my children or any child is racist as well. This is not something we can stand for in our country."[37]

The most publicized protests that caught the attention of the media were at the meetings of the school board in suburban Loudoun County, Virginia, starting in the spring of 2021. Parents were in high dudgeon, demanding that critical race theory lessons be removed from their children's classrooms. The school board, for its part, did not take their suggestions well, displaying a lack of respect for parents by limiting or suppressing their ability to speak. Tempers were so riled that one parent was arrested at a June meeting.

At a June 22, 2021, school board meeting, one parent made a passionate plea to keep these negative ideas out of her children's classrooms: "[S]top teaching little kids that the world is built of these gigantic barriers based on the color of your skin. . . . [T]he school system is using the terms of CRT, 'overlapping vocabulary,' white supremacy and systemic racism."[38]

One of the parents, Ian Prior, announced that he has formed a group called "Fight for Schools" that is gaining wide support within Loudoun County and beyond its borders. The chief project of this group was filing a lawsuit for the recall of six of the school board members.

On October 6, 2021, a first positive opinion was handed down by a Loudoun County circuit court judge: the ruling allows the parents petition to go forward, denying the motion to dismiss by school board member Beth Barts. The judge also agreed to appoint a special prosecutor when the case goes to trial. Mr. Prior stated, "Today we were given a seat at the table and a fair process."[39]

MOBILIZING THE FEDS AGAINST PARENTS

Before that judicial ruling was announced, the National Association of School Boards had already written to the president of the United States to recommend that the actions of some people protesting education policy be classified "as a form of domestic terrorism and hate crimes."[40]

In less than a heartbeat, Attorney General Merrick Garland took up the cause. In a memo on October 4, 2021, he declared the unleashing of the law enforcement apparatus of the state against parents by forging a "partnership along federal, state, local, tribal, and territorial law enforcement to address threats against school administrators, board members, teachers and staff."[41]

What threats? The language in the Garland memo, on its face, is frightening. Rounding up the whole police power of our country, including the FBI, against parents? What have they done but try to speak at school board meetings, to express their disapproval of the curriculum of critical race theory being forced on their children in elementary and secondary schools?

When has the behavior of parents in a public meeting been so twisted as to call it "domestic terrorism" and speaking out on school subjects as a "hate crime?" This is surely an example of overkill. If the president instructed the attorney general to threaten the parents of school children, it will and should be roundly condemned.

Watching the progress of the Loudoun County case and the laws and rulings being pursued in other states is a sort of morality play in progress. For the American family, the content and quality of their children's education is of prime concern, and the ability of parents to engage with teachers, administrators, and school board members must not be abridged, not under our constitution.

Reason has prevailed rather quickly among the leaders of the National Association of School Boards Association. By October 23, 2021, the association published a public apology for the unwarranted language in their letter to the White House: "The NSBA apologized for its letter to President Joe Biden calling for help from federal law enforcement to assist 'with threats and violence from parents and protesters.' . . . [T]here was no justification for the language used in the September 29, 2021 letter."[42]

It was reported in the article cited here that two association members took the liberty of sending the infamous letter to the White House without informing their colleagues for agreement. The White House did confer with the Department of Justice before Attorney General Merrick Garland issued his famous order for federal and state agencies to come down hard on parents at school board meetings.

The National School Board Association took the honest, commendable course in publicly admitting their wrongdoing. No acknowledgment is made by the White House that its Department of Justice overstepped its bounds. Attorney General Merrick Garland declared on October 27, 2021, that no apology was necessary and firmly supported his actions. But the parents in Loudon County, Virginia, and in other school districts across the country are surely taking note.

THE AGENT WHO MADE CRITICAL RACE THEORY KNOWN

Christopher F. Rufo, raised in an Italian immigrant family in Sacramento, California, educated at Georgetown University, is the public face and the undisputedly strongest voice attacking critical race theory. He began his career as a documentary-film maker in remote, exotic locations, then moved into projects on the causes of poverty and homelessness in Seattle, Washington, his home and work site, as well as completing a law degree.

It was in Seattle that he first encountered the new anti-racism programs being provided to city employees. On studying the text of these training programs, he saw the dividing of people into racial groups and that "under the banner of 'anti-racism' Seattle's Office of Civil Rights is endorsing principles of segregationism, group-based guilt, and race essentialism—ugly concepts that should have been left behind a century ago."[43]

The Seattle situation became the wake-up call for Rufo to research the roots of the new anti-racism movement, digging back to the original ideas of radicals of fifty years ago. The usual ideologues—Angela Davis, Paulo Freire, Herbert Marcuse, and others—have been identified earlier in this work as the radicals who influenced today's crop of star activists, Ibram X. Kendi, Robin DiAngelo, and Isabel Wilkerson. It became Rufo's personal and professional mission to make critical race theory popularly understood, and its dangers noticed and opposed.

Rufo's notoriety took off appreciably in the past year or so with interviews in elite venues of wokeness like the *Atlantic* and the *New Yorker* on one side, and citadels of opposition thinking like the *City Journal of the Manhattan Institute* and the *Wall Street Journal* on the other side. Appearing on Fox News for an interview with Tucker Carlson catapulted Rufo beyond the stars and planets to a gig at the Trump White House to assist in the drafting of an executive order, described on the first page of this essay.

The *New Yorker* piece, an interview of Rufo by staff writer Benjamin Wallace-Wells, really is a hit piece, as is abundantly clear from its title, "How a Conservative Activist Invented the Conflict over Critical Race Theory: To

Christopher Rufo, a Term for a School of Legal Scholarship Looked Like the Perfect Weapon," June 18, 2021. But the article allows Rufo to make his points clearly and emphatically to a huge audience, a triumph for him.

He is the fresh face of the anti-CRT movement, arguing against the hyper-elevation of its influence on the workplace, government, and all levels of education especially post George Floyd. Rufo has been consulted by several states to help them draft the language of new laws curbing the use of CRT, including Idaho, Oklahoma, Tennessee, and Texas.

He is busy debunking the myth promoted by progressives that critical race theory is only an abstract idea that has no practical uses or harm in it. He is also attacking the lie that people opposed to critical race theory don't want early U.S. history or anything about racism to be taught in the schools.

Rufo claims these excuses are completely false. State legislation does not ban discussion of racism in the classroom, but it does prohibit teachers from making students believe that one race "is inherently superior to another" or that one race is "inherently oppressive," or that an individual "bears responsibility for actions committed in the past by other members of the same race." The same bills explicitly say that "teachers may and should discuss the role of racism in American history, but they may not shame or treat students differently according to their racial backgrounds."[44]

CONCLUDING THE CONVERSATION

The idea for this essay started with a concern over abstract ideas on the left, such as the new anti-racism, that were beginning to blossom in academia. The dismissal of the principles of Black leaders who had worked and died to bring about a united, respectful-of-all, national community was being strongly delegitimized. The ideas of these earlier Black leaders have been especially eroded in more recent decades.

It was mainly during the new millennium that the forces for publicly shaming Whites and creating racial divisions began commanding our national conversation about rights. The diversity training industry grew and flourished, plying its trade not only in academia but in government agencies, corporations, and schools.

Then came 2020 with the two most consequential events that blew everything out of proportion: the COVID-19 pandemic that locked down our lives and our spirits, and the killing of George Floyd that drove the tolerance for destructive behavior in our major cities. Our world had indeed changed, and not for the better.

NOTES

1. "Presidential Executive Orders concerning Critical Race Theory," *Academic Questions* 34, no. 3 (Fall 2021): 156–177.

2. "Legal Information Institute LII," December 22, 2020: https://en.wikipedia.org/wiki/Legal_Information_Institute.

3. Adam Kirsch, "The Godfather of Critical Race Theory," *The Wall Street Journal*, June 25, 2021.

4. Kirsch, "The Godfather of Critical Race Theory."

5. Craig Frisby and Robert Maranto, "Diversity Training Is Unscientific, and Divisive," *Academic Questions* 34, no. 2 (2021).

6. Musa al-Gharbi, "Diversity Is Important. Diversity-Related Training Is Terrible," *Minding the Campus*, November 6, 2020.

7. Michael Gonzalez, "Progressivism: The Great Transformation in Jeopardy?," *The Heritage Foundation*, July 7, 2021: https://www.heritage.org/progressivism/commentary/the-great-transformation-jeopardy.

8. Christopher F. Rufo, "Intersectional AmEx: The Firm Teaches Employees That Capitalism Is Fundamentally Racist, Then Asks Them to Deconstruct Their Racial and Sexual Identities," *City Journal*, August 11, 2021: https://www.city-journal.org/american-express-company-critical-race-theory-training-program.

9. Christopher F. Rufo, "Walmart vs. Whiteness: The Company's New Training Program Tells Hourly Employees That They Are Guilty of 'Internalized Racial Superiority," *City Journal*, October 14, 2021: https://www.city-journal.org/walmart-critical-race-theory-training-program

10. Rufo, "Walmart vs. Whiteness."

11. Rufo, "Walmart vs. Whiteness."

12. Rufo, "Walmart vs. Whiteness."

13. Chinese American Citizens Alliance Greater New York, "CACAGNY Denounces Critical Race Theory as Hateful Fraud," February 23, 2021.

14. Daniel Asia, "Where Does the University Go from Here," *Academic Questions* 34, no. 2 (Summer 2021).

15. Private communications between Ralph Beals and author.

16. Allen C. Guelzo and James Hankins, "Civilization and Tradition," *The New Criterion* 40, no. 1 (September 2021).

17. Victor Davis Hanson, "Classical Patricide," *The New Criterion* 40, no. 1 (September 2021): 15.

18. "Notable and Quotable: Princeton," *The Wall Street Journal*, September 7, 2021.

19. Hanson, "Classical Patricide," 15.

20. Cornel West and Jeremy Tate, "Howard University's Removal of Classics Is a Spiritual Catastrophe," *The Washington Post*, April 19, 2021, op-ed.

21. Hanson, "Classical Patricide," 15.

22. Bruce P. Frohnen, "Critical Race Theory and the Will to Power," *Academic Questions* 34, no. 3 (Summer 2021).

23. Jason L. Riley, "Correcting 1619's Falsehoods about the American Founding," *The Wall Street Journal*, May 26, 2021.

24. Riley, "Correcting 1619's Falsehoods."

25. Bruce P. Frohnen, "Critical Race Theory and the Will to Power," *Academic Questions*, Summer 2021, vol. 34 - 3.

26. Frohnen, "Critical Race Theory and the Will to Power."

27. Leslie Harris, "I Helped Fact-Check The 1619 Project, *The Times* Ignored Me," *Politico*, March 6, 2020: https://www.politico.com/news/magazine/2020/03/06/1619-project-new-york-times-mistake-122248.

28. David Folkenflik, "After Contentious Debate, UNC Grants Tenure to Nikole Hannah-Jones," NPR, June 30, 2021: https://www.npr.org/2021/06/30/1011880598/after-contentious-debate-unc-grants-tenure-to-nikole-hannah-jones.

29. Robert C. Enlow personal letter to the author, edChoice, September 1, 2021.

30. Robert C. Enlow personal letter to the author, edChoice, September 1, 2021.

31. Tom Fitton, "Mass. School District Segregates Students/Staff Based on Race," *The Judicial Watch*, June 29, 2021.

32. Claremont Institute letter, July 8, 2021.

33. Jason L. Riley, "Critical Race Theory Is a Hustle," *The Wall Street Journal*, July 12, 2021.

34. Riley, "Critical Race Theory Is a Hustle."

35. Riley, "Critical Race Theory Is a Hustle."

36. Michael Brendan Dougherty, "Dewey Defeats Critical Race Theory," *National Review*, July 12, 2021, 20.

37. Dougherty, "Dewey Defeats Critical Race Theory."

38. Hannah Natanson, "How Loudoun County Became the Face of the Nation's Culture Wars," *The Washington Post*, July 5, 2021.

39. Kaelan Deese, "Virginia Judge Allows Parent Group's Forward Motion in Petition to Oust School Board Members," *Washington Examiner*, October 6, 2021: https://www.washingtonexaminer.com/news/virginia-judge-allows-parent-group-forward-motion-in-petition.

40. Deese, "Virginia Judge Allows Parent Group's Forward Motion."

41. Roger Kimball, "Merrick Garland Just Tipped Over the Dominos," *Real Clear Politics*, October 10, 2021: https://www.realclearpolitics.com/2021/10/10/merrick_garland_just_tipped_over_the_dominos_553721.html.

42. Virginia Aabarm, "NSBA Apologizes for Letter Calling Parents 'Domestic Terrorists,'" *Washington Examiner*, October 23, 2021.

43. Benjamin Wallace-Wells, "How A Conservative Activist Invented Conflict over Critical Race Theory" *The New Yorker*, June 18, 2021: https://www.newyorker.com/news/annals-of-inquiry/how-a-conservative-activist-invented-the-conflict-over-critical-race-theory.

44. Christopher F. Rufo, "Battle over Critical Race Theory," *The Wall Street Journal*, June 28, 2021.

8

Concluding Thoughts

We've Gone Too Far

Change is the only constant in human history. It would be futile to attempt to freeze a nation in some admired period in time as the ideal to be maintained. Considering the developments in recent decades, as described in the preceding essays, there is one overarching judgment that applies to all the issues: we went too far.

A brief summarizing of themes, policies that early appeared beneficial but when pursued to excessive levels became negative and harmful to the common good—this would seem to be the best path for turning in a new direction.

Drawing a curtain over one's last large public statements is difficult. The impulse to wax eloquent on every subject is a temptation that must be resisted. Collecting materials, reflecting on major and minor events in our recent national history, the causes and effects, lead to an attempt to understand and present some conclusions and caveats for the readers. There is value in a rational discussion of the demons that plague us today, the events that have brought us to our present concerns. It is fairly simple to identify the forces dangerous to the continued viability of our country. Promoting that discussion is the serious priority of this work.

There have been extremely difficult times throughout our history. When our country was in its infancy and early youth, there were exterior and interior events that might have stunted or completely nullified our ability to become the constitutional republic we are. We overcame them all to various degrees, not to a state of perfection.

Our nation moved forward through cycles of warfare and accommodation with first settlers of the continent, early arrivals seeking religious freedom, slaves from Africa, immigrants seeking work and opportunity. Was there ever a time of calm equanimity, of peaceful coexistence in our country or in the wider world? That would be a relative, individual judgment.

Chapter 8

THE ECONOMY AND THE NEW TECHNOLOGIES

The American economy grew and prospered fairly consistently from the 1950s on, with intermittent periods of financial crisis, most recently in the severe downturn in 2009. The United States, with its Marshall Plan that helped rebuild the countries destroyed in World War II, invested enormously in the economic development of third-world countries, and to nation building, with varying degrees of success.

During that same period, American industry gradually collapsed and manufacturing moved overseas, creating pockets of unemployment detrimental to the working class. The imbalance of powerful corporations moving overseas for profit has benefited our trading partners, principally China, but has yet to produce a comparable benefit for the working class in our own country. New employment is almost entirely in tech-related industries, and the promise of retraining unemployed workers from service jobs and long-gone heavy manufacturing—it's just not happening enough.

American ingenuity created new technologies in Silicon Valley that produced major changes in all areas of business, professional, and personal life—instant communication, instant news, instant personal relations, and constant entertainment. Over time the technologies have become more intrusive, invasive of privacy, and capable of generating destructive social movements.

The negative impact on freedom of speech, the easy path for political intimidation, cancel culture, and self-censorship are now increasingly evident. The negative aspects of instant communication, given the power of the conglomerates in control, are almost impossible to curb. During the current pandemic, there are reports of the damaging effects on young people spending an inordinate number of hours daily on social media platforms. How much more controlling new technological advances will be may be determined by some future youngsters dreaming and experimenting in a backyard garage or at MIT.

WOMEN, MEN, AND SEX DISCRIMINATION: CULTURAL CHANGES OF CONSEQUENCE

In the last quarter of the twentieth century, women's liberation flourished, especially in middle-class communities of well-educated women. Great strides were made in opening access to higher education, professions, elective offices at every level, and corporate positions of leadership. In academia, a mini-affirmative action mood prevailed for women to become tenured faculty in greater numbers and to rise in administrative positions. Elite colleges and universities rose admirably to the challenge.

In the schools of education, where teachers are trained to instruct our children, a clamor arose to undo the unfair practice of ignoring girls in the classroom. Apparently, girls were not being called on enough to speak up. In mathematics and science classes, especially, classroom speech always seemed to be dominated by boys. Much fuss was made for a few years with teacher training programs striving for a reset.

At the same time a great deal of attention was invested in identifying children with special needs who deserved special help in the classroom to keep up with lessons being taught. This might look like individual tutoring, small group lessons, or being allowed more time in test taking. In extreme cases, the remedy was the medication of students or assignment to a special school, at no cost to the family. The Individuals with Disabilities in Education Act (IDEA) was passed in 1970 to lend federal guidelines and resources.

These two separate endeavors, over time, have had adverse effects on a few generations of boys. Christina Hoff Sommers of Clark University in her book *The War against Boys: How Misguided Feminism Is Harming Our Young Men* (2000) provides a scathing account of the effects on young boys. Between the dictum that girls needed a lot more attention in the classroom, and the emergence of a system bent on classifying boys as a problem, attitudes inimical to the growth and educational flourishing of boys into men settled in.

The special education industry grew every year to identify more and more students in need of their services, and the majority were boys. They were prescribed medication at an early age for the new attention-deficit/hyperactivity disorder (ADHD) prognosis. What had been earlier considered normal behavior in the classroom for active young boys was now classified as a special education problem, needing "behavior modification." Watching this work its way through the schools in Newton, Massachusetts, over a decade made us pause to wonder how earlier generations of children ever learned anything without all of these enhancements.

Feminism of the classic early variety achieved most of its stated goals some time ago and has gone through various styles of activism from its 1970s appearance on the national scene. We are a much better country for it. Have we achieved a truly level playing field between the sexes? Not for the men of our country.

Men in this millennium are thoroughly marginalized, stigmatized, and in many ways are failing or at serious risk. This need not have been the case. As women have flourished, expanding their presence in every arena they choose to compete in, there was no imperative that they had to demean and diminish the other sex—but it has been intentionally done.

Without belaboring the point about inequity, that is, that men have higher suicide rates, drug addiction rates, and are routinely called out and publicly shamed (if White), the attention here will be focused on the loss of male students at the college level. In the 2021 college enrollment figures, 59.5 percent are women and 39.5 percent are men, often cited in the press as a 60/40 split, when rounding the figures.

A study of college enrollments by race and family income level reports that at every level White, Black, Asian, and Hispanic men are in clusters of almost equal percentages not attending college. White men's enrollment rate isn't much higher and is often lower than minority men in the same income group. The analysis of U.S. Census Bureau Population Survey data by Tom Mortenson of the Pell Institute for the Study of Opportunity in Higher Education should shake the foundations of the common assumptions about "White Male Privilege" so prevalent in 2022.

The Mortenson analysis was included in a front-page *Wall Street Journal* investigative report in September 6, 2021, "A Generation of American Men Give Up on College: 'I Just Feel Lost,'" by Douglas Belkin. Among the key points highlighted,

- the education gap has been widening over the past forty years with no reversal in sight;
- highest gap of female/male enrollment is at private, four-year colleges;
- skyrocketing costs make college less affordable and risk of future debt a greater concern; and
- female students benefit from a support system of clubs, women's centers on campus (almost none exist for men).

Belkin's comprehensive report acknowledges that some colleges are taking covert steps to bring more young men to their schools. The overwhelming efforts that get publicity on campus are the harassment of women students and the racial inequity problem. No school would dare to risk being publicly outed for inviting more male enrollment in this era of gender politics. An enrollment consultant quoted in the Belkin article speaks sense on the matter:

[The conventional view on campuses is that] men make more money, men hold higher positions, why should we give them a little shove from high school to college? . . . If you care about our society, one, and, two, if you care about women, you have to care about the boys, too. If you have equally educated numbers of men and women that just makes a better society, and it makes it better for women.

Best to conclude the discussion of the imbalance of the sexes in American society at this point in time. There is, however, one other noteworthy change over the last half dozen years. The major consolidation of higher education into coed colleges and universities and military academies is mirrored by a comparable change in most high schools, both public and private, since the 1970s. According to Wikipedia, there now remain a total of three all-male colleges and a total of thirty-five all-women colleges in the United States.

GENDER IDEOLOGY: RADICAL FEMINISM TO LGBTQ+

The last example of going too far related to radical feminism is in the explosion of transgender numbers in the past decade, the types of nonbinary identities, and the prescribed language to accommodate them all. It is the attempt to deny human biology, and it is succeeding, due to the complicity of the medical establishment, the compliant media, and the fear instilled in parents by the radicals in these groups.

In truth, adults who decide to undergo medication and surgery to change their birth sex do not present a problem needing public attention. The growth and power of gender ideology that is deeply troubling is in these areas: giving young children early access to puberty blockers; the huge increase in teenage girls claiming "gender dysphoria," and the assault on women's sports and safe spaces.

Abigail Shrier, author of *Irreversible Damage: The Transgender Craze Seducing Our Daughters* (2020) delivered data essential to an understanding of this subject on April 27, 2021, at a Hillsdale College National Leadership Seminar. Shrier describes these basic data of crucial importance:

- most young children exhibiting discomfort with their biological sex are boys; if left alone (not medically treated), 70 percent naturally outgrow their gender dysphoria;
- in the past decade, a broad campaign to accept as valid the early imposition of puberty blockers in young children has been easily encouraged and is firmly in place;
- the number of teenage girls electing to pronounce themselves "trans" has so increased as to be labeled a social contagion;
- girls as young as thirteen are allowed to start treatments that will eliminate their future fertility and sexual function, without parental approval, even on a first visit;
- these treatments are not reversible; no data yet prove the benefits of transgender procedures to the individuals who have undergone "gender affirming therapy";

- anti-women's rights in sports and privacy: biological males on girls' sports teams, no protective spaces for women in restrooms, locker rooms, prisons.

The harm to boys and girls is real and well-documented in the Shrier research. These ill-considered movements need severe curbing, through laws restricting the procedures to adults, or to young people in consultation with parents, medical doctors, and psychologists. There is an ancient witticism that applies to the subject of human biology, perhaps by an English teacher (author unknown): nouns have gender; people have sex.

The rights of women to their own sports teams and privacy must be restored. Women fought hard to gain recognition for their own teams on the playing fields and should not sit still for this blatant intrusion on their territory. Removing the private space of women's public bathrooms is so ludicrous and insulting as not to merit discussion. There is no question we have gone too far here.

ON RACE AND EDUCATION

These two subjects are investigated and expanded on *ad infinitum* in the preceding chapters. It is never too late to add a few good thoughts to end the discussion on an inspiring note. The first choice is to provide two elegant quotes from Frederick Douglass, provided by Bari Weiss in the November 2021 issue of her online commentary podcast *Politics and Ideas*. The first is this: "Education means emancipation. It means light and liberty. It means the uplifting of the soul of man into the glorious light of truth, the light only by which men can be free."

The second Frederick Douglass quote is the motto of his anti-slavery paper the *North Star*: "The Right is of no Sex—Truth is of no Color—God is the Father of us all, and all we are brethren."

Arkansas Representative Mark Lowery asked the attorney general of the state if the teaching of critical race theory in the schools is in any way against the law:

"Yes, it is," said Attorney General Leslie Rutledge. "Any effort that takes account of race, that gives benefits or opportunities differently or creates a hostile environment in an education institution is unlawful. The Equal Protection Clause and Title VI teaching that certain traits or beliefs are proper to individuals of some races but not others, that an individual, simply by virtue of race is oppressive or oppressed, and should feel either guilt or distress. Of course, you can talk about our country's history of the Civil War and Jim Crow . . . in any critical discussion of historical events."[1]

Former secretary of state Condoleezza Rice engaged in a remarkable event, a respectful exchange with Whoopi Goldberg, one of the hosts of the TV program *The View*. Fans of this program know it to be a famous venue for extremely heated diatribes on all manner of discussions touching on "woke" subjects. Rice, a Black woman who grew up in the segregated south, gave us a simple, clear statement, free of academic jargon. Her advice on the racial divide is that we must not degrade one party in order to benefit another:

> It is important for both black and white children to grow up feeling empowered, and for black children not to be taught that their white schoolmates are racists, and for the white students to not be made to feel like they should have to shoulder the guilt of bad things that happened in our nation long before they were born.[2]

THE COVID-19 EFFECT

Trillions of words will be written about this era before it ends—if it ever does end. The national, local, and personal impact of this pandemic on all countries and people is the most consequential health scare we have experienced since the worldwide flu contagion a hundred years ago. Confusion, apathy, annoyance on the one side, and on the positive side, genuine examples of heroic behavior of health care workers, service employees, and parents of school children, who have kept the world on as steady a course as possible.

The year 2020 gave us the canceling of in-person education at all age levels, rationing of in-person health care to prioritize care of COVID-19 sufferers, shortages of basic goods, restrictions on travel and social gatherings—all deemed essential for controlling the spread of the virus. At the political level, there have been policies based on predictions that were proven wrong, the official reluctance to admit the obvious genesis of the virus in a Wuhan, China, lab, and the effects of lockdowns on the economy and on social dislocations.

It may be determined, in the future, that our leaders probably erred in subjecting the entire country to lockdown rather than focusing the most severe measures on the most vulnerable populations (the elderly in nursing homes, people with compromised health) and allowing less stringent polices for places with lower rates of infection. All of this is open for debate, but the one indisputable achievement of 2020 is the development of the vaccines by several pharmaceutical companies. Giving inoculations to millions of people, beginning in December 2020, is a historical event of tremendous importance to the health of the entire world.

At the personal level, the period of lockdown, face masks, and distancing could not help but deepen cultural and generational isolation, and the over reliance on our machines for "connecting." Increasing the reliance on virtual reality, especially for the young, has had damaging effects with increased rates of depression, drug use, and suicides.

On display for the whole world to note, the deplorable behavior of high public officials who promoted the most severe restrictions on all aspects of life but were then observed flouting the very rules they mandated. The examples are legion and were on television news programs: governors of California, Michigan, Illinois, big city mayors, all the way up to the speaker of the House of Representatives and her beauty salon escapade.

When laws do not apply to those who make them, people are not being governed, they are being ruled. This topic will conclude with the observations of an Illinois judge who ruled in favor of a small business owner against Governor Pritzker's shutdown order:

> Since the inception of this insanity, the following regulations, rules or consequences have occurred: I won't get COVID if I get an abortion but I will get COVID if I get a colonoscopy. Selling pot is essential but selling goods and services at a family-owned business is not . . . . If I go to Walmart I won't get COVID but, if I go to church, I will. The defendant in this case (the Governor) orders you to stay home and pronounces that, if you leave the state, you are putting people in danger, but his family members traveled to Florida and Wisconsin because he deems such travel essential . . . .. These are just a few examples of rules that are arbitrary, capricious and completely devoid of anything even remotely approaching common sense.[3]

COURAGE TO REIN IN THE CULTURAL REVOLUTION'S POWER

Are there enough wise and courageous leaders in academia, in the medical profession, in the corporate world, and in government—enough people sufficiently distressed with the dilemma of our country—who will now begin to stand tall and oppose the untruths, not meekly but with active resistance?

When a counterfactual history such as the 1619 Project is published, it is the responsibility of a greater number of historians to attack and publicly oppose it. When students and faculty cruelly "cancel" a professor with blatant misrepresentations, there must be many more on our campuses to speak out forcefully to defend the person unjustly pilloried. When any leader, Black or

White, states that nothing has changed in recent decades in the opportunities and resources for minorities, authentic facts must be loudly proclaimed to overturn the lies.

When every single person is consigned to a group identity, and group hatred is promoted in the diversity training programs, it must be opposed by business leaders and government officials. No individual in this country should ever be forced to apologize for his or her skin color or ethnicity or so-called "privilege."

Opposing public lies requires courage. It may be that as each display of truth-telling is broadcast, a few more people will stiffen their backbones and take the risk of speaking out, but advisedly in a civil manner, not in the mode of the antifa barbarians. The "Silenced Majority" must rediscover its strength in numbers.

Emily Bobrow, writing for the *Wall Street Journal*, identifies one supremely courageous individual. Pano Kanelos, the former president of St. John's College, has embarked on the Herculean task of creating a new college. He is raising funds to open his University of Austin in Texas (UATX) to enroll its first freshman class in fall 2024. His aim is to offer, "the kind of affordable, intellectually rigorous, ideologically heterodox, experience . . . which is increasingly rare in higher education today."

LAST WORDS

The serious issues addressed here come together to form a multifaceted reality of five decades of changes. Coming to terms with the opposing forces affecting us and the positives and negatives of each on family, economic circumstances, schooling, self-realization, social culture, and politics—the challenge is daunting. The explosion of mass communications technology bears a heavy responsibility for making us far too "connected." Trying to digest the masses of information flooding our brains may be keeping us off balance and struggling to understand the world and our local part in it.

There is a persistent fear that the political ideas and related laws that are most potentially damaging to our commonwealth—the re-imposition of racial and ethnic segregation in the name of equity, the obsession with tribal distinctions more than on individuals—these are the elements that are dividing our country most fiercely today. The ideal of an integrated polity, of a population united in mutual respect across differences of color and ancestry, these ideals prevailed for a few decades from the 1960s to the new millennium but are barely recognized today.

The new ideal on the far left is to return to considering racial identity as the *sine qua non,* the anti-White intolerance coupled with radical impositions on freedom of speech and thought. That these trends should be most vigorously and unthinkingly promoted in the universities, in the name of eradicating racism, augurs a more disruptive future if left unchecked.

In the traditional sense of what America has often demonstrated to the world, whenever perilous conditions have confronted the nation, a positive spirit emerges to counter the forces of negativity and revive a return to good sense, balanced rights, and responsibilities. There are signs that an awakening number of courageous leaders are confronting the "woke" morass of current social and political culture, not to turn back the clock to a mythical utopia, but to reverse the effects of perilous progressivism, to a moderate, centrist ideal.

> "I believe order is better than chaos, creation better than destruction. I prefer gentleness to violence, forgiveness to vendetta. On the whole, I think knowledge is preferable to ignorance, and I am sure that human sympathy is more valuable than ideology."
>
> —Sir Kenneth Clarke, Civilization, PBS Masterpiece Theater.

NOTES

1. "Critical Race Theory in universities likely violates federal law, legal analysis," *The College Fix*, August 25, 2021: https://www.thecollegefix.com/bulletin-board/critical-race-theory-in-universities-likely-violates-federal-law-legal-analysis/.

2. Sister Toldjah, "Condi Rice Stuns 'View' Hosts with Knockout Argument Against Critical Race Theory," *Red State*, October 20, 2021: https://redstate.com/sister-toldjah/2021/10/20/inject-into-my-veins-condi-rice-stuns-view-hosts-with-knockout-argument-against-critical-race-theory-n459963.

3. Judge Michael McHaney, "Americans Don't Get Ruled," RealClearPolitics, May 27, 2020: https://www.realclearpolitics.com/articles/2020/05/27/americans_dont_get_ruled_143306.html.

4. Emily Bobrow, "Pano Kanelos: A College President Hopes to Chart a New Path for Higher Education, " *Wall Street Journal*, Weekend Confidential, January 29–30, 2022, C9.

Bibliography

Ayvazian, Andrea. "Are We an Enclave of 'Nice Racists'"? *Daily Hampshire Gazette*, September 18, 2021: https://www.gazettenet.com/Guest-columnist-Andrea -Ayvazian-42481274.

Belkin, Douglas. "A Generation of American Men Give Up on College: 'I Just Feel Lost.'" *Wall Street Journal*, September 6, 2021: https://www.wsj.com/articles/ college-university-fall-higher-education-men-women-enrollment-admissions-back -to-school-11630948233.

Bell, Derrick. *Faces at the Bottom of the Well: The Permanence of Racism.* New York: Basic Books, 2018.

Corvino, John, Ryan T. Anderson, and Sherif Girgis. *Debating Religious Liberty and Discrimination.* Oxford UK: Oxford University Press, 2017.

Delgado, Richard, and Jean Stefancic. *Critical Race Theory: An Introduction.* Third edition. New York: New York University Press, 2017.

DiAngelo, Robin. *White Fragility: Why It's So Hard for People to Talk about Racism.* Boston: Beacon Press, 2018.

———. *Nice Racism: How Progressive White People Perpuate Racial Harm.* New York: Penguin Random House, 2021.

Douthat, Ross. "The West and What Comes After." *New York Times*, July 8, 2017: https://www.nytimes.com/2017/07/08/opinion/sunday/the-west-and-what-comes -after.html.

Fukuyama, Francis. *The End of History and the Last Man.* New York: Simon & Schuster, 1992.

Glazer, Nathan. *Affirmative Discrimination: Ethnic Inequality and Public Policy.* Cambridge, MA: Harvard University Press, 1987.

Glazer, Nathan, and Daniel Patrick Moynihan. *Beyond the Melting Pot: The Negroes, Puerto Ricans, Jews, Italians and Irish of New York City.* Cambridge: M.I.T. Press, Harvard University Press, 1963.

Hoff Summers, Christina. *The War against Boys: How Misguided Feminism Is Harming Our Young Men.* New York: Simon & Schuster, 2000.

Huntington, Samuel. *The Clash of Cultures and the Remaking of World Order.* New York: Simon & Schuster, 2011.

Kendi, Ibram X. *How to Be an Anti-Racist.* New York: Penguin Random House, 2020.

Kimball, Roger. *The Long March: How the Cultural Revolution of the 1960s Changed America.* San Francisco: Encounter Books, 2000.

Leeming, David. *James Baldwin.* New York: Alfred A. Knopf, 1994.

Leven, Yuval. *A Time to Build: From Family and Community to Congress and the Campus, How Recommitting to Our Institutions Can Revive the American Dream.* New York: Basic Books, 2020.

Liptak, Adam. "The Supreme Court Seems Poised to Uphold Mississippi's Abortion Law. *New York Times,* December 1, 2021: https://www.nytimes.com/live/2021/12/01/us/abortion-mississippi-supreme-court.

Loury, Glenn C. "A New American Dilemma." *The New Republic,* 1984: https://www.academia.edu/596293/A_new_American_dilemma.

Murray, Charles. *Facing Reality: Two Truths about Race in America.* New York: Encounter Books, 2021.

Porter, Rosalie. *Forked Tongue: The Politics of Bilingual Education.* New York: Routledge, 1994.

Porter, Rosalie P. *American Immigrant: My Life in Three Languages.* Piscataway, NJ: Transaction Publishers, 2011.

Powell, Mike. "Inside a Battle over Race, Class and Power at Smith College." *The New York Times,* February 24, 2021: https://www.nytimes.com/2021/02/24/us/smith-college-race.html.

Riley, Jason L. *Maverick: A Biography of Thomas Sowell.* New York: Basic Books, 2021.

Shrier, Abigail. *Irreversible Damage: The Transgender Craze Seducing Our Daughters.* Washington, DC: Regnery Publishing, 2020.

Styron, William. *The Confessions of Nat Turner.* New York: Random House, 1967.

Thiessen, Marc A. "On Abortion, the Supreme Court Is Set to Overturn Decades of Wrongs." *Washington Post,* December 2, 2021: https://www.washingtonpost.com/opinions/2021/12/02/abortion-supreme-court-kavanaugh-plessy-mississippi/.

Wallace-Wells, Benjamin. "How a Conservative Activist Invented the Conflict over Critical Race Theory." *The New Yorker,* June 18, 2021: https://www.newyorker.com/news/annals-of-inquiry/how-a-conservative-activist-invented-the-conflict-over-critical-race-theory.

Wilkerson, Isabelle. *The Warmth of Other Suns: The Epic Story of America's Great Migration.* New York: Random House, 2010.

———. *Caste: The Origins of Our Discontents.* New York: Random House, 2020.

Wood, Peter W. *The 1620 Project: A Critical Response to the 1619 Project.* New York: Encounter Books, 2020.

Woodson, Robert L., Sr. *Red, White and Black: Rescuing American History from Revisionists and Race Hustlers.* New York: Simon & Schuster, 2021.

Woodward, Kenneth L. *Getting Religion: Faith, Culture, and Politics from the Age of Eisenhower to the Era of Obama.* New York: Convergent Books, 2016.

About the Author

Dr. Rosalie Pedalino Porter is the author of *American Immigrant: My Life in Three Languages* (2011); *Language and Literacy for English Learners: Grades 7–12, Four Programs of Proven Success* (2004); and *Forked Tongue: The Politics of Bilingual Education* (1990; second edition, 1996).

She began her professional career as a Spanish/English bilingual teacher in the Springfield, Massachusetts, public schools and was director of the bilingual/ESL department in the Newton, Massachusetts, public schools from 1980 to 1990.

Porter has served as an expert witness in court cases relating to the education of non-English-speaking children in Arizona, California, New Mexico, New York, and Texas. She lectured on education policies for immigrant children under the sponsorship of the U.S. State Department in Bulgaria, China, Finland, Israel, Italy, Japan, and Turkey. In *Flores v. Arizona*, a case in which the U.S. Supreme Court ruled in favor of Arizona in 2009, Porter's research was cited in the ruling.

She holds undergraduate and graduate degrees—BA (magna cum laude), MEd, and EdD—from the University of Massachusetts/Amherst, spent a year as a visiting scholar at the University of London, and was a research fellow at the Radcliffe Institute for Advanced Study at Harvard University, 1987–1988. The Fulbright Commission of the U.S. State Department appointed Dr. Porter to a lectureship on English language teaching in Rome, Italy, for the 1992–1993 year. In 1997 she was awarded a research residency at the Rockefeller Study Center, Villa Serbelloni, on Lake Como, Italy.

As a child, Porter arrived in the United States at age six, knowing not a word of English.

CPSIA information can be obtained
at www.ICGtesting.com
Printed in the USA
LVHW110359300622
722206LV00006B/219

9 781475 865332